Making
DOUGH

This book is dedicated to my father, who always taught me to pay attention in math and science because it would prove valuable in life. Little did I know I would one day be the person in the story problems who buys 98 pounds of butter, 180 pounds of flour, 50 pounds of sugar, and 82 apples.

Library of Congress Cataloging in Publication Number: 2014956802

ISBN: 978-1-59474-818-9

Printed in China
Typeset in Brandon Grotesque and Sentinel

Designed by Andie Reid

Photography by Russell van Kraayenburg, except for the following pages by Mason van Kraayenburg: 4, 26, 40, 48, 70, 86, 98, 116, 132, 150, 158, 176, 192, and 202

Production management by John J. McGurk

Quirk Books
215 Church St.
Philadelphia, PA 19106
quirkbooks.com

10 9 8 7 6 5 4 3 2 1

Making
DOUGH

RECIPES AND RATIOS *for*
PERFECT PASTRIES

RUSSELL VAN KRAAYENBURG

QUIRK BOOKS
PHILADELPHIA

CONTENTS

INTRODUCTION

Pastries, and the doughs that give them life, have a daunting reputation. Their intricate construction, precise recipes, and time-consuming techniques can keep even the most adventurous home cooks from attempting to make them. But they are not as complicated as they sound!

I'd like to share a secret that professional pastry chefs have known for years: you need to know only a dozen dough recipes to be able to make countless pastries. Galettes, hand pies, pot pies, and crackers all use the same recipe for pie dough. Doughnuts, cinnamon rolls, brioche à tête, and rolls can be made from brioche dough. And the same recipe for shortcrust dough is the foundation for savory tarts, dessert tartlets, pop tarts, and even some cookies. Regardless of the application, the methods for preparing each of these twelve doughs remains the same; a croissant is a croissant, no matter your time zone.

With the help of this book you can master these twelve basic pastry doughs: biscuit, scone, pie, shortcrust, sweetcrust, pâte à choux, brioche, puff pastry, rough puff pastry, croissant, danish, and phyllo. You will also find instructions for 82 pastries and variations that use the basic doughs, plus 30 recipes for fillings, toppings, and glazes. Mix and match the doughs, techniques, fillings, toppings, and sauces for innumerable possible pastries—all from just a handful of simple dough recipes.

WELCOME TO THE WORLD OF PASTRIES

I've always been obsessed with the inherent simplicity of baking. And I've been baking for as long as I can remember, trying to capture and create the magic of some of my favorite pastries. Their simple construction—often nothing more than butter, flour, and water—becomes the base for so many flavors, a doorway to a never-ending variety of pastries.

The first time I baked was in the backyard. My primary ingredient? Mud. I can remember the mix of defeat and pride on my mother's face every time she had to buy a new pie pan because one of hers had mysteriously disappeared. The first time I baked in a real kitchen, it was, to my parents' disapproval, without adult supervision. I vaguely remember adding more baking soda

than flour to my concoction and using a few Cheerios for texture. The result came out green.

Eventually, my baking exploits became more commonplace. Everyone in my family had a sweet tooth, and indulging it became a family affair. And though in the beginning our cookies came from plastic containers, our biscuits from cardboard tubes, and our cakes from boxed mixes, we slowly began to expand our horizons. Soon we tried biscuits from scratch. Cakes whose batter we mixed according to a recipe. Eventually, our cookies more often came from the ingredients in our fridge and pantry, not a squishy tube. My father started making his own crepes. But our pastries—boy, did we like our pastries—were purchased from local bakeries and pastry shops. We never dared to make those from scratch. We didn't even prepare our own pie or tart crusts. They were simply too difficult. Or so we thought.

After nearly a decade of living, and cooking, on my own—missing home-cooked meals and desserts from scratch—I began to explore the world of pastries that I once found too intimating and attempted to make homemade pastries easy and accessible. I'm glad I did, and I hope you will be, too. Let's get started!

GETTING STARTED

With this book I hope to help you make delicious, from-scratch pastries at home. First we'll look at the science and math behind baking to discover how altering the ratio of ingredients can produce wildly different results. Once we've explored the different types of dough, we will form them into different shapes and mold them into distinct baking dishes, and then mix and match them with a variety of fillings and toppings. The possibilities are endless.

Each of the twelve basic dough recipes can be boiled down to a simple ratio of five numbers—the amounts of flour, fat, liquid, sweetener, and egg. You can use that ratio to customize any dough—scale it to your needs or substitute ingredients to make your own recipes. Understanding these ratios makes from-scratch pastries easy and, more important, a lot of fun.

WHAT IS DOUGH?

Every kind of dough contains flour and a liquid (usually water or milk). It may also contain fat (butter, lard, shortening, bacon fat, etc.), sugar or other sweetener (honey, maple syrup, corn syrup, etc.), a leavener (yeast, baking soda or powder, air, etc.), eggs, salt, and flavorings. Dough is any amalgamation resulting from the combination of those ingredients—unless it's a batter. Batters are similar to doughs, but they can be poured and are typically used to make waffles and pancakes, muffins, cakes, and other delicate desserts. We're not worried about batters here. This book is all about doughs—the ones you can work with your hands.

What distinguishes one dough from another is the relationship between its ingredients. For example, pie dough, biscuit dough, and puff pastry dough contain the same three primary ingredients: flour, butter, and a liquid. But by altering the amounts, you can create vastly different crumb sizes, textures, and flavors (consider the difference between a dense bacon cheddar biscuit and the ethereal layers of mille-feuille).

Pastry baking takes more than just a carefully measured combination of ingredients, though. You also need to combine the ingredients in just the right way. Mixing method is what allows us to control the texture, weight, and sturdiness of a dough. If a dough's ingredients are like the building materials at a construction site, the ratio is the blueprints and the mixing method is the construction team. The rest depends on the tools you use and the flavorings you add.

The Missing Doughs

The scope of this book is pastry dough, which means that, in addition to batters, a few other types of doughs are not discussed. The first is pasta dough; at its simplest this mixture contains only water and flour, but recipes may include eggs and fat. Also omitted is bread dough, a category so vast and varied that it truly deserves its own book (though brioche is covered here; see page 117).

Terms

The following pastry terms are used frequently throughout this book.

Baked good: the pastry after it has been baked.

Crumb: the final texture of a baked good.

Fat: the butter, lard, or shortening used in dough to add flavor and assist in creating texture.

Flavoring: any ingredient used to influence how a dough tastes, such as vanilla extract or spices.

Flour: ground grain or cereal.

Gluten: a protein developed by mixing flour with a liquid. It creates a dough's basic structure.

Lamination: a technique in which many layers of alternating dough and butter are created through rolling, turning, and folding.

Leavening: a specific ingredient, or a byproduct of mixing, that incorporates air into a dough before or during baking to influence texture.

Liquid: water, milk, juice, or other fluid used to aid in the creation of gluten, add flavor, and/or contribute to texture.

Ratio: a numerical representation of the relationship between the amounts of ingredients used in a recipe.

MEASURING

There are three ways to measure when baking. The first is visually: simply throw things into a bowl. This is the least advisable method. The second is by volume—this is how you've probably been measuring since you were a little kid baking alongside your mother, using those stacked cups and spoons. The third method is to by weight (or, technically speaking, mass), which is done using a scale. You should use the third method.

Measuring ingredients by mass is more precise than measuring by volume, because different ingredients have different textures and densities. One ounce of sugar takes up nearly half the space of one ounce of flour and therefore has almost half the volume (put another way: 1 cup of sugar weighs roughly 8 ounces, but 1 cup of flour weighs roughly 4 ounces). More importantly, though, volume can vary greatly depending on if the ingredient you're measuring has been compacted into a container, how it is scooped, and even how long it has been sitting in your pantry; this is especially true of flour and brown sugar. For this reason, volumetric measuring can be very imprecise, and successful pastries require precision.

Don't take my word for it, though. Try this simple test: Using a spoon, gently scoop flour from the bag into a 1-cup measuring cup. Fill it completely, but make sure not to press the flour into the cup. Then lightly scrape the top of the cup with a knife to level the flour. Pour the flour into the bowl of a kitchen scale and record the weight. Next, repeat the test, but instead of scooping the flour into the cup, draw your measuring cup through the bag of flour, lightly pressing the flour in the cup with your palm. If your experiment is like mine, the second cup of flour will weigh nearly an ounce more than the first. That's a substantial difference. For the most accurate measuring for baking recipes, always weigh dry ingredients.

MEASURING BY SIGHT?

While I don't advocate measuring large quantities of flour with your hand, you may find it handy—pun intended—to memorize what ½ teaspoon or 1 teaspoon of salt looks like in your palm. The same goes for baking soda, powder, sugar, and any other ingredients that you regularly use in small amounts.

RATIOS

I know, I know: ratios mean math. But knowing the ratio of ingredients in a dough recipe will not only help you scale it to the yield you want (and easily convert recipes from metric to American customary—see page 202—or from volumetric measuring to mass-based measuring), it will help you understand the differences among the various doughs in this book. When you see an 8:7:2 ratio of flour to butter to water, you know you can throw 8 ounces of flour in a bowl, cut in 7 ounces of butter, and mix in 2 ounces of water to get a delicious pie dough. You'll also know you can do the same thing with 16 ounces of flour, 14 ounces of butter, and 4 ounces of water—or 2 cups of flour, ³⁄₄ cup plus 2 tablespoons of butter, and ½ cup of water—and still form the same mixture. Math. Who knew it was so helpful!

Baking with ratios is nothing new. In fact, the most common method for recording a recipe in a professional kitchen, the baker's percentage, is based on ratios. According to the baker's percentage, the amount of flour in a recipe (no matter the amount) is always recorded as 100%. Then each ingredient is recorded as a percentage based on its weight relationship to the flour. So if a recipe calls for 2 ounces of sugar and 8 ounces of flour, the sugar would be recorded as 25%. As helpful as this method is when cooking on a large scale, it's a bit complicated for home cooking. For our purposes, ratios are simpler.

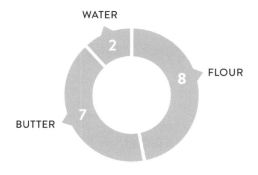

WATER
2
FLOUR
8
BUTTER
7

INGREDIENTS

Doughs comprise up to five primary ingredients: flour, fat, eggs, liquid, and sugar or another sweetener. Not every dough includes all five, but you'll find many of them in the doughs in this book. The relationship between the amounts of these ingredients is what define each dough recipe and distinguish one dough from another. Other ingredients include leavening and salt, which are vital, and flavorings, which aren't vital but do make baked goods delicious.

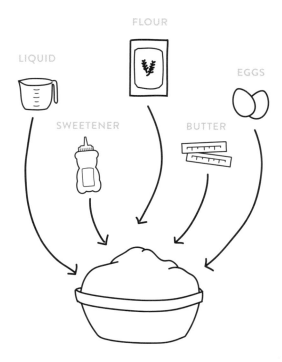

FLOUR

LIQUID

EGGS

SWEETENER

BUTTER

Flour

Flour is a ground meal of grain, typically wheat, or sometimes nuts or even vegetables. The proteins, starches, and fiber found in flour can produce different results depending on their interaction with the other ingredients in a recipe. This versatility makes flour a star ingredient in cooking and the base of all doughs. But what does flour actually do?

1. The proteins in flour (glutenin and gliadin) bind with water to create gluten, the primary structure in dough. This allows dough to rise into a particular shape during baking. The protein in flour also affects the final texture of a baked good.

2. The starch in flour, when cooked, supports the structure created by the gluten and its interaction with leavening agents. This lets a baked good hold its shape after baking.

3. Flour contributes flavor to the dough.

4. When combined with liquid, the starches in flour act as a thickening agent for fillings, sauces, and gravies.

5. The natural sugars in flour caramelize during cooking, creating color and texture.

Now that you know what flour does, let's look at different kinds of flours and their uses. The biggest difference among them is the protein content: Flours high in protein will create baked goods with a chewier texture, while flours lower in protein will contribute a softer texture.

Types of Flours

A flour's protein content directly affects the gluten formed in the dough. More protein means more gluten, and more gluten means a more rigid texture. Mixing time also affects gluten formation: doughs that are mixed only briefly develop little gluten, while doughs that are mixed or kneaded for minutes will have more.

FLOUR TYPE	PROTEIN CONTENT	BEST USE
CAKE FLOUR	6–8%	Biscuits, Sweetcrust Dough
PASTRY FLOUR	7–10%	Puff Pastry, Croissants, Danishes
ALL-PURPOSE FLOUR	9–12%	Scones, Shortcrust Dough, Croissants, Brioche dough
BREAD FLOUR	11–15%	Pie Dough, Scones, Brioche Dough, Pàte à Choux, Phyllo, Puff Pastry
WHOLE WHEAT FLOUR	10–18%	Bread Dough, Rich Pastries

So which flour should you use? I suggest keeping your pantry stocked with both bread and cake flours. You can use either on its own or create your own mix. The recipes in this book call for either a specific mixture of these two or for just one or the other. (A 1:1 or 3:2 mixture of bread flour to cake flour will roughly emulate all-purpose flour; a 2:3 mixture of bread flour to cake flour will roughly emulate pastry flour.) But you can substitute all-purpose flour for the flour in any of these recipes. Just be sure to substitute it 1:1 for the full flour content.

Other Grain Flours and Nut Flours

Flours can be made from grains other than wheat as well as nuts, and each creates a flavor that bread or cake flour alone cannot create. Oat flour, barley flour, almond flour, and even pecan flour can be used in baking. I recommend substituting them for up to 20% of the wheat flour called for in a recipe and, for the rest, stick with a mixture of bread and cake flour.

Storage

Despite its incredible powers, flour is as vulnerable as almost any other ingredient. It contains a small amount of water, and over time it can either dry out or absorb moisture from the air. Some flours, such as whole wheat flour (which has a high water content and retains oils from the grain), can turn rancid quickly. When you open a paper sack of flour, transfer it to an airtight container—with as little room for air as possible. Keep flours in a cool, dry, dark place, such as a pantry or cabinet far from your oven.

Although I never have flour long enough for it to reach its expiration date—it usually is baked within a couple of weeks of entering my pantry—I suggest using refined white flours within six months of purchase, whole wheat flours within one month, and ground nut flours within a week. If you grind or mill the nuts and grains yourself, I suggest using the flour immediately or freezing it in an airtight container. If you don't use flour often, buy it in small quantities. And, of course, my general rule of thumb for any ingredient is if it smells bad, don't use it.

Liquid

In addition to building gluten in the dough, liquid can affect a dough's flavor.

Water

Water is the most common liquid used in making doughs. Its taste varies from one municipality, brand, or filter to another, and this taste can be pronounced in baking. Filtered water will give your baked goods the cleanest, least offensive taste.

Milk

With a small fat content, milk adds richness to baked goods and a familiar, creamy dairy flavor that water cannot. You can substitute water for milk—or milk for water—in nearly any baked good.

However, be careful when using milk in yeast-risen doughs. Because milk contains proteins that can retard or even kill yeast, it should be heated to 140°F and then cooled before being mixed into a yeast dough. This will allow the dough to rise better and under more controlled circumstances than if you were to simply dissolve the yeast in unheated milk.

Lemon Juice

Unlike milk, lemon juice should not be substituted for water. It is used in small amounts in baking because of its acidic properties. Here's what it does:

1. It activates baking soda in doughs.

2. It stabilizes egg whites in meringues.

3. It counters excess sweetness.

4. It imparts sourness.

5. It can make sugar-based recipes (jams, syrups, etc.) sweeter.

When a recipe calls for lemon juice, squeeze juice from a lemon. Avoid the bottled stuff.

Fat

Another important ingredient in doughs, especially layered pastry doughs, fat is integral to the structure and texture of a baked good, and it adds flavor.

Texture

In pie crusts, biscuits, puff pastries, croissants, and danishes, fat is a textural superstar. Rather than being blended uniformly into these doughs, it is purposely kept separate. In pie dough and biscuits, it is left as little dots and strips throughout the dough; in puff pastry, croissants, and danishes, it forms paper-thin ribbons between layers of dough of the same thickness. As the dough bakes, the fat evaporates, acting as a leavening agent and fluffing the dough up slightly. When it has evaporated completely, the fat leaves only two things: flavor and empty air between the layers of dough. This process is what creates the flaky texture common to these types of baked goods.

In doughs that are kneaded, such as brioche, the fat is incorporated in order to encourage elasticity and flexibility. And in doughs that are barely mixed, such as shortcrust, fat contributes a smooth, tender, crumbly texture.

Flavor

Fat also adds flavor, and for baking, butter may be the best, most flavorful fat you can use. More strongly flavored fats like bacon fat and certain oils don't always pair well with other ingredients in baked goods, and although lard and shortening are more effective than butter at creating a flaky texture, their flavor is inferior, so I opt not to use them. Additionally, both also have a higher melting point than butter. This can keep them from being readily absorbed into a dough, which can result in baked goods that leave a strange film in the mouth when eaten.

Eggs

In dough recipes that call for them, eggs are fundamental. Here's what they do:

1. When whipped or creamed, eggs aid in leavening baked goods.

2. Eggs emulsify liquids and oils, two ingredients that otherwise do not combine.

3. Eggs support a dough's structure during baking, allowing starches in flours to retain structure after baking.

4. Eggs help suspend fat molecules in batters and doughs, which keeps these mixtures from becoming greasy.

5. In custards and creams, eggs provide flavor and can act as thickening agents.

6. Like fats, eggs help baked goods retain moisture, extending a baked good's shelf life.

7. Eggs affect a pastry's appearance. Egg whites lend a lighter, white color. Egg yolks lend a darker, yellow hue.

8. Egg washes act as glue to seal pastries together and also add color to baked goods.

There are countless egg substitutes available, but none come close to being able to do everything that the real thing does.

Storage

Although eggs may be stored at room temperature, refrigeration quadruples their life (eggs at room temperature can last a week, and eggs left in a refrigerator can last up to a month or more). Eggshells are porous and will absorb flavors from the surrounding environment, however, so store them in either their original package or an airtight container. Separated or unshelled mixed egg whites and egg yolks should be stored in an airtight container in the refrigerator. Egg yolks must be used the same day the egg is opened; whites can be stored, refrigerated, for up to a week. Combined eggs can be stored for up to three days. If you are worried about freshness, remember my rule: if it smells bad, don't use it.

Size and Quality

Egg size can vary greatly. I use large "Grade A" eggs as a basis for measuring in this book. They weigh on average, without the shell, about 1¾ ounces. (Yolks weigh about ½ ounce, whites a little more than 1 ounce, and shells about ⅔ ounce to 1 ounce).

If you halve a recipe that calls for 1 egg, simply whisk 1 egg in a bowl and use half of the mixture in the recipe.

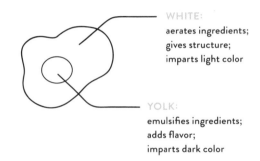

WHITE:
aerates ingredients;
gives structure;
imparts light color

YOLK:
emulsifies ingredients;
adds flavor;
imparts dark color

Sugar and Sweeteners

These ingredients, like the others used in doughs, are veritable jacks-of-all-trades. The benefits that sweeteners provide are not the same, so honey or corn syrup should not be substituted for sugar in equal quantities. If it isn't obvious already, this isn't a healthy cooking book. You cannot use chemical sugar substitutes in place of sugar in baking and expect the same results.

Sugars

Raw, brown, granulated, and powdered sugars caramelize when heated, influencing a baked good's color and flavor. Sugar can also leaven and aerate mixtures when creamed with butter and eggs. In yeast doughs, sugar feeds the yeast, which creates air bubbles and lightens the dough. In meringues, sugar adds structure and delays deflation.

Lastly, sugar is hygroscopic, meaning it attracts and retains moisture. This quality of sugar helps extend the shelf life of a baked good and preserves recipes like jams and jellies. Sugar's moisture retention can promote mold growth, so it should be stored in an airtight container. It can last almost indefinitely, but I suggest keeping it around for no more than a year.

Granulated sugar is the most commonly used sugar. It is highly refined from either sugar canes or sugar beets. (I prefer baking with refined cane sugar.) If you like to avoid refined, processed foods, you can substitute raw sugar 1:1 for white sugar.

Brown sugar often comes in two varieties, light and dark. Most brown sugar is simply refined white sugar that has had molasses added to it; light brown sugar has less molasses than dark. The molasses makes brown sugar acidic and thus will activate baking soda—granulated sugar will not. The molasses in brown sugar will create a softer, darker baked good than will granulated sugar. Brown sugar can be substituted for up to 50% of the white sugar in a recipe though it may affect flavor.

Powdered sugar is refined granulated sugar that has been pulverized into a fine powder. Cornstarch is often added to it to keep it from sticking to itself. Powdered sugar should not be used in place of granulated or brown sugar. It is used primarily in frostings and glazes, where the gritty texture of other sugars is undesirable.

Honey

Honey is more flavorful than refined sugars, and its flavor can vary depending on the flower from which it is made.

Because it is a liquid sweetener, it creates a moister baked good than sugar. Its high moisture content and hygroscopic attributes also help extend a baked good's shelf life.

Like other liquid sweeteners, honey will help delay and prevent crystallization of sugars in syrups and caramels. It can be used to glazed baked goods, although it has a lower caramelization point than sugar and can burn.

Honey is best substituted for sugar in batter recipes, but it can replace up to 10% of the sugar in most doughs. In some cases, you may need to add extra flour to offset the added moisture.

Corn Syrup

Corn syrup is rarely found in home kitchens these days. It can be used as a stabilizing agent in caramel and various sauces and syrups. I use it in only a few recipes for which its helpful attributes are essential.

Molasses

Molasses, in addition to being an ingredient in brown sugar, is used to flavor recipes, especially gingerbread cookies and cakes. Strongly flavored, it should be used sparingly.

Maple Syrup

Maple syrup has a distinct flavor that is often a welcome addition to cakes, cookies, fillings, and sauces. In doughs it should not be substituted 1:1 for sugar (or even for honey, which is more viscous than maple syrup).

Salt

Salt helps accentuate other flavors, especially sweet ones, and it affects both the texture and the color of baked goods. In yeast-risen doughs, it will slow fermentation. Salt also can strengthen proteins, giving gluten more power to support a loaf of bread or other baked good and allowing whipped egg whites to hold their shape longer.

There are a lot of salts on the market. For recipes in this book I recommend kosher salt, a larger-grain salt that contains no additives.

Flavorings

Some ingredients' sole purpose is to flavor a baked good. They include vanilla—extract, bean, or paste—liquors, chocolate, nuts and nut butters, spices, herbs, and fruits and vegetables.

Vanilla

I use vanilla to flavor many fillings and sauces. From the fruit of the *Vanilla* genus of orchid plants, it comes in three forms: bean (fruit), paste, and extract. Good extract is expensive, but because it is used sparingly, a bottle should last a long time. My preferred extracts are bourbon vanilla and Mexican vanilla (both come from the same variety of plant). Never use imitation vanilla.

The vanilla bean, or pod, is the dried, intensely flavorful fruit of the vanilla plant. I use whole beans—split open to expose their seeds—to make vanilla custard and ice cream. Vanilla beans provide recipes with a wonderful flavor as well as tiny, distinctive black seeds. Once used, vanilla beans can be rinsed, dried, and added to sugar to make vanilla sugar.

Vanilla bean paste is vanilla extract mixed with vanilla bean seeds, so it, too, adds those characteristic black flecks to recipes. You can substitute it 1:1 for vanilla extract. For recipes that call for a whole vanilla bean, you can substitute 1 teaspoon vanilla paste or extract.

Liquors and Extracts

Liquors, such as spirits like rum and whisky, can flavor recipes, as can extracts, which come in various fruit and nut flavors. Don't use them in place of other liquids in doughs, however. Save them for sauces and fillings (where they can be substituted for vanilla extract).

Chocolate

Quality chocolate, like vanilla, can be expensive. When buying chocolate, be sure to buy bars that are free of additives, and avoid chocolate chips, which contain emulsifiers that help them keep their shape but aren't suitable for most baking.

Nuts and Nut Butters

Ground nuts and nut flours can replace up to 20% of the total flour called for in dough recipes. But nut butters, such as almond butter or cashew butter, cannot take the place of butter in dough recipes. However, they may be swapped with peanut butter in fillings and sauces.

Spices

Spices are rarely used in dough, except for some yeast doughs. More often they are found in fillings and sauces. If you do not like a spice, you can simply omit it without altering a recipe.

Leavening

Ingredients known as leaveners create pockets of air in baked goods, such as the irregular spaces in a French baguette; such pockets give different recipes their distinctive texture and crumb. There are three types of leavening: mechanical, chemical, and natural.

Mechanical Leavening

Mechanical leavening simply means that the mixing method employed in a recipe functions as the leavening. Biscuit, puff pastry, croissant, danish, shortcrust, and sweetcrust doughs are leavened mechanically. (Croissant and danish doughs are leavened also with yeast, a natural leavener. Biscuits are leavened with an additional chemical leavener.)

Leaving fat in chunks throughout the dough or folded into neat layers between dough is the mechanical leavening method behind pie, biscuit, scone, puff pastry, croissant, and danish doughs; during baking, the fat dissolves and air pockets are left behind.

Chemical Leavening

The two most popular chemical leaveners are baking soda and baking powder. Both products contain sodium bicarbonate, an alkaline compound that reacts with liquids and an acid to produce carbon dioxide. This produces little air bubbles that create texture and crumbs.

BAKING SODA VS. BAKING POWDER

What's the difference? Baking soda is simply sodium bicarbonate. In order to work, it must be combined with both a liquid and an acid. It begins working as soon as these ingredients are mixed, so recipes using baking soda must be baked immediately.

Baking powder, on the other hand, contains baking soda (sodium bicarbonate) plus two acid powders (typically monocalcium phosphate and sodium aluminum sulfate). Thus, baking powder requires only the addition of a liquid to work.

Each acid powder allows the baking powder to work twice, first when the liquid is introduced and second when heat is introduced. This is how "double-acting baking powder" gets its name.

You don't have to bake products with baking powder immediately, but they will rise better if you do.

Natural Leavening

By natural leavening, we mean yeast, a living organism that produces carbon dioxide as it eats. In essence it does the same thing as baking powder or baking soda, but it's far more finicky and requires more work and understanding. However, it yields greater rise and a distinctive earthy flavor. (Too much baking soda or baking powder can also flavor a baked good, but not in a good way.)

Yeast can work only in certain temperatures, between 40°F and 140°F, but is most active between 80°F and 90°F. Temperatures above 140°F kill it, and temperatures below 40°F render it dormant. Yeast thrives on sugar (both natural sugars found in ingredients and granulated sugar), and salt will retard its carbon dioxide–producing capabilities or kill it outright if the yeast comes in direct contact with it.

Yeast is sold in three forms: fresh, instant, and active. Fresh yeast is highly perishable, making it fairly impractical for home baking. Instant yeast doesn't need to be dissolved in a liquid before using. It is unsuitable for the recipes in this book, because it acts too quickly to allow for proper rising and proofing. Active yeast comes in granular form, usually in little packets or jars, and it must be dissolved in liquid before use. Use active yeast in all the recipes in this book calling for yeast.

TOOLS

Every recipe in this book can be made by hand. In some, using a food processor or stand mixer makes the process easier. I provide instructions for both methods. I encourage you to try each recipe by hand at least once, because getting a feel for the dough, literally, will help you understand the dough's characteristics.

Some other tools and equipment, like baking dishes, are essential, and others will make your life easier. You probably already have most of these in your kitchen.

MARBLE SLAB

Marble slabs retain cold very well—after 20 minutes in the freezer, they stay cold to the touch for at least an hour, and in some dough recipes a chilled work surface is indispensable. Marble is slick and relatively nonstick, and marble boards require slightly less flour than cutting boards to prevent dough from sticking. They don't retain odors or flavors like cutting boards do. Lastly, they are very easy to scrape clean with a pastry scraper and to wash with a sponge and lightly soapy water.

PARCHMENT PAPER

Parchment paper is wonderful. It can be used to line baking sheets to prevent sticking and make cleaning easier, wrapped around doughs for storage, and even laid down on surfaces for rolling and kneading.

The Must-Haves

Most of these are multipurpose, affordable, and likely already in your kitchen.

rolling pin

chef's knife

paring knife

serrated knife

whisk

spoons

pots

bowls

cooling racks

kitchen scale

measuring cups

measuring spoons

candy thermometer

pastry brush

ruler

Microplane

Tools That Make Things Easier

Although not required in the recipes, these tools will make baking much simpler.

sieve

bench scraper

vegetable peeler

pastry cutter

biscuit cutters

propane torch

piping bags and tips

icing spatula

Work Surfaces

A good work surface is key for making dough. It should be at least 1½ by 2 feet. Options include a countertop, cutting board, or marble slab.

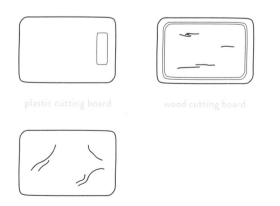

plastic cutting board

wood cutting board

marble slab

Baking Dishes

You will need at least one of each of these dishes if you want to try every recipe in this book.

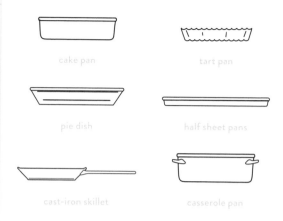

cake pan

tart pan

pie dish

half sheet pans

cast-iron skillet

casserole pan

The Mechanized Monsters

Mixing dough by hand is an experience I encourage you to try, but undoubtedly a stand mixer and a food processor make this process a breeze. The ice cream maker is used only once in this book but is essential if you want homemade ice cream.

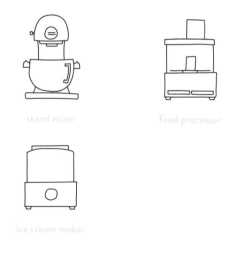

stand mixer

food processor

ice cream maker

MIXING METHODS

The mixing method is the process by which you combine various ingredients to form a dough. About ten exist, but only five are needed to make the doughs in this book.

One-Stage Method

This is the simplest mixing method: combine all of the ingredients at once and mix until blended. Do this by hand on a flat surface, with fingers or a spoon in a bowl, or in the bowl of an electric mixer fitted with a paddle attachment and running on medium-low speed.

USED FOR: Puff pastry dough, puff pastry butter block, croissant butter block, danish butter block, phyllo dough

Biscuit Method

In this mixing method, chunks of fat are not fully incorporated with dry ingredients but rather cut, chopped, or pinched in the flour mixture until broken up. Do this using your fingers, a dough cutter, pastry scraper, food processor, or stand mixer fitted with the paddle attachment. The texture of the mixture should be pea-sized pieces for pie dough, rough cornmeal for biscuits, or fine sand for shortcrust. Add the liquid and mix carefully, just enough to form a dough while still keeping the fat separate.

The temperature of the fat varies. Biscuit, scone, and pie doughs use cold butter; shortcrust uses softened, room temperature butter. In recipes in which cold fat is required and you are working with your hands, be aware that your body heat may raise the temperature of the butter, which makes it harder to keep separate from the flour.

USED FOR: Biscuit dough, scone dough, pie dough, shortcrust dough, rough puff pastry dough

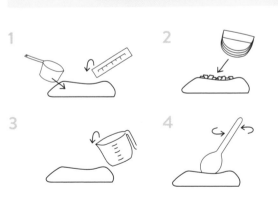

Biscuit Bowl Method

Biscuit Food Processor Method

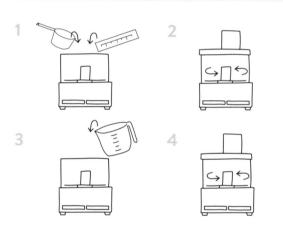

Biscuit Mixer Method

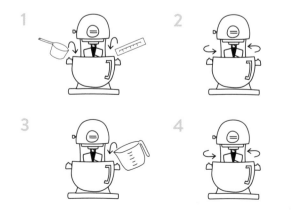

Pâte à Choux Method

Pâte à choux is made by an amalgamation of processes. To begin, bring water and butter to a boil. Then reduce heat to medium-low and add flour, mixing thoroughly. Once a dough forms, remove the pot from the heat and add the eggs one at a time, mixing each in completely. Mix the dough until it is elastic and shiny.

Adding the flour to the water and butter must be done on the stove, but mixing in the eggs can be done by hand or with the paddle attachment of an electric mixer on medium-low speed.

USED FOR: Pâte à choux dough

Pâte à Choux Hand Method

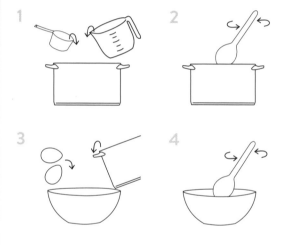

Pâte à Choux Mixer Method

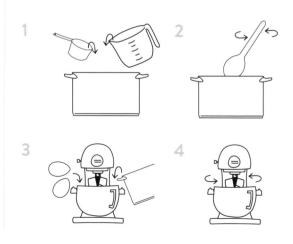

Straight Dough Method

The straight dough method is not unlike the one-stage method, though it is used to make yeast-leavened doughs only. First, dissolve the yeast in warmed liquid (between 105°F and 110°F). Next, add all the remaining ingredients to the bowl. Then knead the dough with a stand mixer fitted with a dough hook (the speed and time depends on the dough), and finally leave it to rest or rise, depending on the dough.

USED FOR: Brioche dough, croissant dough, danish dough

Straight Dough Hand Method

Straight Dough Mixer Method

Poolish Dough Method

This mixing method adds an extra fermentation step to the straight dough method, which yields a dough with additional flavor. A portion of the liquid, yeast, and flour is mixed together and set aside to rise and develop flavor (anywhere from a couple of hours to a day). It is then kneaded into the remaining ingredients to form a dough. The dough is then kneaded (shorter for danishes and croissants, longer for brioche dough). After that, the dough is left to rise (for brioche) or rest before folding (for danish and croissant dough).

USED FOR: Brioche dough, croissant dough, danish dough

Poolish Dough Hand Method

Poolish Dough Mixer Method

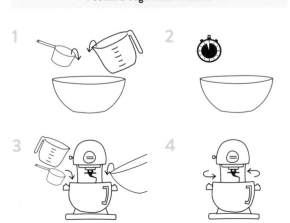

TIPS FOR WORKING WITH DOUGH

The technical steps required to work with dough (mixing, kneading, rolling, shaping) can seem overwhelming. Here are some tips and tricks to make working with dough a breeze.

Preparing

It is always a good idea to read through a recipe at least once before starting it, so you know what you will be doing and the kitchen equipment required. I also recommend measuring all the ingredients before starting to prepare a recipe. It will make the work quicker and easier.

Mixing

You'll see plenty of terms for combining ingredients, including *stir*, *mix*, *beat*, *whisk*, and *whip*. Each means something slightly different. *Stir* means to gently combine with a spoon using a circular motion. *Mix* is a more vigorous stir, also with a spoon. *Beat* is the most intense type of stirring; it is used to break up or incorporate ingredients such as sugar and butter. Beating is easiest with an electric mixer fitted with a paddle attachment, but it can be done by hand with a spoon. *Whisk* means a slow to moderate stir using a whisk. *Whip* means to combine quickly and vigorously so as to aerate ingredients. Whipping is easiest with an electric mixer fitted with a whisk attachment, but it can be done by hand with a whisk.

Kneading

Kneading is a form of mixing. It develops the gluten in dough, and it distributes the ingredients evenly. It is usually reserved for the toughest of the doughs.

1  Work dough into a rough ball and set on a lightly floured surface. Dust the top of the ball and your hands with flour.

2   Using the heel of your palm, push down and away from you on the center of the dough ball.

3 Fold the pushed flap over top of the ball.

4  Rotate the ball 90 degrees. Using the heel of your palm, push down and away from you on the center of the dough ball again. Fold the pushed flap on top the ball. Repeat.

Rolling

I suggest using a French rolling pin (the kind with tapered edges and no handles), because it gives you the most control. To reduce fatigue, place your hands, fingers open, on top of the rolling pin at each end. Start with the rolling pin at your fingertips and roll until it reaches the heels of your palms. Avoid rolling past your palm to your arms.

Rolling a Circle

Rolling a circle can be quite tricky to do but becomes easy with practice. The secrets are to use consistent pressure and to constantly rotate the dough as you work.

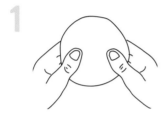

Form dough into a rough circle with your hands. Place on a lightly floured surface and lightly flour the top. Rub flour on the rolling pin.

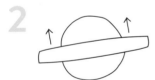

Roll from the center of the dough away from you.

Rotate dough an eighth of a turn (45 degrees), and roll again from the center away from you. Repeat until you achieve the desired thickness and size.

TIP *If the dough begins to split at the edges, use the tapered side of the rolling pin to roll each split portion toward the other until they touch and fuse back together.*

Rolling a Rectangle

Rolling a rectangle is a little easier than rolling a circle, but pay attention at the corners to ensure the shape stays a rectangle with each roll.

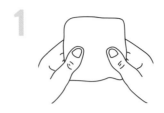

Form dough into a rough rectangle with your hands. Place on a lightly floured surface and lightly flour the top. Rub flour on the rolling pin.

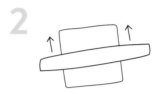

Roll from the center of the dough away from you.

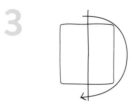

Rotate the dough a half turn (180 degrees) and, again starting from the center, roll away from you.

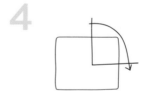

Rotate the dough one quarter turn (90 degrees) and, again starting from the center, roll away from you. Repeat steps 2–4 until you reach the desired thickness and size.

TIP *If the corners begin to curve or you lose the rectangular shape, roll from the center to the corner at a 45-degree angle to push the corner out.*

MAKING IT YOUR OWN

Here is where baking gets fun. The magic, and secret, to baking is understanding that all you need are 12 ratios, a little flour, butter, and water (and sometimes some eggs, sugar, and yeast). Here are some ways to get creative.

Serving Size

Recipes can be doubled easily. Most recipes can be divided in half as well. For puff pastry, croissant, and danish doughs, note that smaller batches are difficult to manipulate, and recipes that are more than doubled are easier to handle when divided into portions.

Substitutions

You can modify doughs by changing the flours and fats used. Try making biscuits with bacon fat or duck fat, or pie dough with a mixture of whole wheat, oat, and white flours. You can even replace some of the flour in sweetcrust dough with cocoa powder, or add lemon zest to croissant dough.

To substitute flours, you must take into consideration the protein content of the flour. Simply replacing all the white flour with whole wheat flour will create a very dense, unsavory product. In general, replace no more than 20% of the flour called for with specialty flours. This rule applies to whole grain, nut, and other high-protein flours or textured flours as well low- and no-protein flours, such as cornstarch.

Substituting sugars and sweeteners can be tricky as well. Sugar is the only readily available solid sweetener, so stick to it whenever it is called for. Always avoid sugar-free, chemical sweetener powders—they cannot perform the same duties as sugar. In shortcrust doughs, you can substitute up to 20% of the sugar with brown sugar, honey, or syrup—this will create a darker, more floral crust.

With fats you have more leeway (except when making puff pastry, croissant, and danish doughs, which rely on butter for both texture and flavor). With few exceptions, stick to solid fats in recipes that call for a solid. Only yeast doughs can tolerate liquid oils substituted for solid fats. Try experimenting with lard, bacon fat, or even duck fat in pie crusts, biscuits, and scones.

Mix and Match

You can have a lot of fun mixing and matching the various doughs, fillings, sauces, and toppings you'll find in this book. Enjoy!

BISCUIT DOUGH is a chemically leavened dough that is made using the biscuit-mixing method. It has a relatively high ratio of liquid to flour and fat. The high moisture content creates a tender, flaky pastry with cakelike texture. It is less dense than the texture of pie dough, which is created using a different ingredient ratio but similar mixing technique. The dough ratio is **8 FLOUR** : **3 FAT** : **5 LIQUID** .

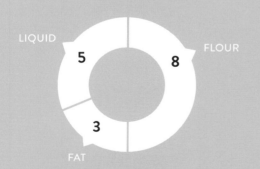

LIQUID
5
FLOUR
8
3
FAT

6 **OUNCES CAKE FLOUR**

2 **OUNCES BREAD FLOUR**

3 **OUNCES BUTTER**

5 **FLUID OUNCES MILK**

Use this dough to make:

Biscuits
Shortcake
Cobbler
Grunt
Biscuits & gravy

BISCUIT DOUGH

YIELD: 1 pound | **PREP TIME:** 20 minutes | **BAKE TIME:** 12 minutes

6 ounces cake flour

2 ounces bread flour

1 teaspoon salt

4 teaspoons baking powder

3 ounces (6 tablespoons) unsalted butter, cold

½ cup plus 2 tablespoons milk

MIXING THE DOUGH

There are two ways to mix biscuit dough: by hand or using a food processor.

By-Hand Method

1. Mix flours, salt, and baking soda in a large bowl.

2. Chop butter into ½-inch cubes. Add to flour mixture.

3. Using your fingers or a pastry cutter, pinch or cut butter into flour, breaking it into pieces about the size of coarse cornmeal. If using your hands, work quickly to prevent butter from melting.

4. Add milk and stir 10 to 20 times with a wooden spoon, until dough just begins to come together.

5. Place dough on a very lightly floured surface. Knead 4 to 5 times, until it just holds its shape. Take care not to knead the dough too much or add too much flour, which can make the biscuits tough.

Food Processor Method

1. Pulse flours, salt, and baking soda in the bowl of a food processor to combine.

2. Chop butter into ½-inch cubes. Add to flour mixture. Pulse for 1 to 2 seconds 8 to 12 times, until mixture resembles coarse cornmeal.

3. Add milk and pulse 2 to 4 times, until dough begins to come

together. It will form a few large chunks and many small ones.

4. Transfer dough chunks to a very lightly floured surface and push together. Knead 3 to 5 times, until dough just holds its shape. Take care not to knead the dough too much or add too much flour, which can make the biscuits tough.

Storage

Bake immediately, or store in an airtight container. Refrigerator: 2 days. Freezer: 1 month.

Qualities of Good Biscuit Dough

THE DOUGH: Biscuit dough should be dry but easy to manipulate. You should also see small dots of butter throughout the dough.

THE PASTRY: Once baked, biscuits should be tender. The outside crust should be firm and crumble easily, and the crumb inside should be soft.

MAKING CLASSIC BUTTER BISCUITS

Position a rack in the center of the oven and preheat oven to 425°F. On a lightly floured surface, roll prepared dough with a rolling pin until ¾ inch thick. Cut out 2½-inch disks with a cookie or biscuit cutter, or simply pull off small handfuls of dough for a more rustic look. Stack pieces of leftover dough, roll dough again, and cut out more disks. Repeat until all the dough is used. Place biscuits on a parchment paper–lined baking sheet spaced at least 1 inch apart. Brush tops with melted butter. Bake for 12 minutes, until tops are just golden. Let biscuits cool on the pan for 1 minute before transferring to a wire rack. Serve warm.

WHY CAKE FLOUR?

The American South enjoys a growing season that is relatively long and free of harshly cold weather, so less hardy varieties of wheat can be grown there. The resulting flour has a lower protein content, which is responsible for the cakey biscuits associated with that region. The similarly low protein content in cake flour will consistently produce these classic soft biscuits.

HOW TO HANDLE LEFTOVER DOUGH

When using a cookie or biscuit cutter to cut out round biscuits, you'll inevitably have leftover dough. Instead of kneading the leftover pieces together before rerolling the dough, stack them in layers and then roll the stack. Every time you knead or roll dough, it will become tougher. Stacking it helps delay the toughening.

ADDING MIX-INS

Throwing in some mix-ins—such as herbs or spices, lemon zest, a small pile of cheese, or a big pile of bacon—is a snap. Biscuit dough can handle it! So long as your add-ins are dry, they won't affect the dough ratio.

DROP BISCUITS

1

Pull off about ⅙ of dough.

COOKIE-CUTTER BISCUITS

1

Roll dough into a rough
rectangle about ¾ inch thick.

2

Use a 2½-inch cookie cutter
to cut out dough disks.

LAYERED COOKIE-CUTTER BISCUITS (AKA PULL-APART BISCUITS)

1

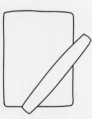

Roll dough into a
12-by-10-inch rectangle.

2

Fold dough four
times to layer it.

3

Use a 2½-inch cookie cutter
to cut out dough disks.

BISCUIT DOUGH RECIPES

BOURBON-MAPLE GLAZED CHEDDAR BACON BISCUITS

2:1:1

THE RECIPE Bacon-cheddar biscuits are always a favorite! This version, inspired by a spur-of-the-moment idea from a friend, is one of the best I've ever tasted. The biscuits are savory and salty. The sauce is rich, earthy, and sweet. This combination is a perfect example of pastry dough used in a savory application.

THE RATIO This recipe has a 2:1:1 ratio of dough to mix-ins to sauce.

1. Preheat oven to 425°F. Heat a griddle to 375°F or heat a large flat skillet over medium heat. Cook bacon for about 25 to 30 minutes, flipping with tongs every 5 minutes, until crispy. Transfer to a paper towel–lined plate. Once cool enough to handle, chop into fine pieces.

2. Meanwhile, bring maple syrup, bourbon, and thyme to a boil in a small saucepan. Reduce heat to maintain a slow boil and cook for about 10 to 15 minutes, until liquid is reduced by a third. Set aside.

3. Prepare biscuit dough according to the instructions on page 28, adding chopped bacon and grated cheddar to the dry ingredients in step 1. Pull dough apart with your hands into 6 chunks and arrange them on a parchment paper–lined baking sheet.

4. Bake for about 12 minutes, until biscuits just begin to turn light golden. Remove thyme sprigs from infused syrup and discard. Brush biscuits with glaze while they are still warm and serve.

YIELD: 6 biscuits

PREP TIME: 45 minutes

BAKE TIME: 12 minutes

1 pound Biscuit Dough (page 28), prepared as at left

6 ounces uncooked bacon

1 cup maple syrup

1½ fluid ounces (3 tablespoons) bourbon

30 sprigs fresh thyme

2 ounces extra-sharp white cheddar cheese, grated

VARIATION

DINNER BISCUITS For simpler, fully savory biscuits, serve these without the glaze. Brush each with melted butter and top with a little extra cheese before baking.

BLACKBERRY MINT SHORTCAKES

1:1

THE RECIPE Blackberries and mint may not sound like ingredients that play well together, but a little cream mellows the strong flavors and makes this pair one of my favorite combinations. In this dessert, they top a standard biscuit for an inspired riff on berries and shortcake. The mint-infused whipped cream alone makes this recipe worth trying.

THE RATIO This recipe has a 1:1 ratio of dough to toppings.

1. Preheat oven to 425°F. Cut biscuits and bake according to the instructions on page 28, about 12 minutes or until lightly golden. Set aside.

2. Heat heavy cream and mint sprigs in a small saucepan over medium-high heat, until cream reaches the scalding point (180°F on a clipped-on thermometer); it will begin to steam and appear slightly frothy. Transfer to the refrigerator and let steep for 1 hour, until cold.

3. Meanwhile, prepare the blackberry sauce: bring pureed blackberries, half of the sugar, chopped mint, lemon juice, and vanilla to a boil in a medium saucepan. Reduce heat slightly to maintain boil and cook for about 3 to 5 minutes, until thickened. Strain liquid through a fine-mesh sieve into a bowl; discard any blackberry seeds. Set aside to cool.

4. Strain steeped cream through a fine-mesh sieve into a large mixing bowl; discard mint leaves. Whip cream with an electric mixer on high speed while slowly adding the remaining sugar, until stiff peaks form. Note: This will take longer than normal whipped cream, up to 10 minutes, because of the oils from the mint leaves. Set aside in the refrigerator.

5. Assemble the shortcakes: Cut biscuits in half to create two rounds. Cover each bottom half with blackberries and blackberry sauce. Top with the top halves. Spoon whipped cream on top and drizzle with a little more blackberry sauce before serving.

YIELD: 6 shortcakes

PREP TIME: 1 hour

BAKE TIME: 12 minutes

1 pound prepared Biscuit Dough (page 28)

1 cup heavy cream

5 sprigs fresh mint

4 ounces granulated sugar, divided

12 ounces blackberries, pureed, plus 12 ounces whole berries

1 tablespoon fresh mint leaves, finely chopped

½ teaspoon lemon juice

½ teaspoon vanilla extract

CINNAMON PORT PLUM COBBLER

1:3

THE RECIPE Cobblers, crumbles, crisps, buckles, brown betties, and grunts are a family of delicious fruit-filled desserts. Crumbles and crisps have a cookie-like crumble topping, buckles have a streusel topping, and brown betties are layered. Topped with biscuit dough, cobblers and grunts are my favorite.

THE RATIO This recipe has a 1:3 ratio of dough to filling.

1. Position a rack in the center of the oven and preheat oven to 400°F. Mix plums, port, granulated sugar, 1 teaspoon of the cinnamon, and cornstarch in a large bowl. Pour mixture into a 10-by-6-inch (or similar sized) baking dish, and bake for 20 minutes. Remove from oven and keep oven on.

2. Pinch off small handful-size clumps (about 2 inches in diameter) of biscuit dough and scatter them on top of the filling so that the clumps touch one another. Brush each clump with melted butter. Sprinkle biscuits with brown sugar and the remaining 1 teaspoon cinnamon.

3. Bake for another 20 minutes, until biscuits are golden brown on top and filling is bubbly. Let cool slightly before serving.

SERVING SUGGESTION

Cobblers, especially those made with rich, tart fruits, pair well with Vanilla Bean Ice Cream (page 108). The cinnamon and port in this cobbler also pair well with richer ice cream flavors like lemon, cinnamon, and chocolate.

PORT FOR DESSERT

Port is a sweet fortified wine often served as a dessert wine. With flavors ranging from rich and sweet to nutty and oaky, it doesn't only go well alongside dessert, it's great *in* many desserts. This recipe's combination of port, spicy cinnamon, and tart, sweet plums is especially good.

YIELD: 1 (10-by-6-inch) cobbler

PREP TIME: 20 minutes

BAKE TIME: 40 minutes

1 pound prepared Biscuit Dough (page 28)

3 pounds plums, pitted and cut into wedges

1 fluid ounce (2 tablespoons) port

2 ounces granulated sugar

2 teaspoons ground cinnamon, divided

1 ounce (¼ cup) cornstarch

1 ounce (2 tablespoons) unsalted butter, melted

1 ounce brown sugar

GRILLED PEACH COBBLER Preheat oven to 400°F. Skin, halve, and pit 2 pounds peaches. Grill peaches over medium-high heat for 5 minutes, until soft and lightly charred. Mix with 8 ounces granulated sugar, 2 tablespoons lemon juice, and 2 ounces all-purpose flour. Place in a 10-by-6-inch baking dish. Proceed with recipe at left, omitting the final 1 teaspoon cinnamon.

BLUEBERRY GRUNT Preheat oven to 400°F. Mix 1 pound mashed blueberries, 1 pound whole blueberries, 2 cups water, 1 pound granulated sugar, and 2 tablespoons lemon juice in a 10-inch cast-iron skillet. Bring to a slow boil over medium-high heat and cook for about 10 minutes, until thickened. Mix 2 ounces (½ cup) cornstarch and ¼ cup water in a small bowl. Add to filling and stir. Return to a boil and cook for another 30 seconds, until thick. Proceed with recipe at left, starting with step 2, transferring skillet directly to oven to bake.

DUCK FAT BISCUITS WITH TARRAGON GRAVY

THE RECIPE I've updated traditional biscuits and gravy, the popular Southern breakfast dish, by replacing the butter in the biscuits with duck fat, which gives them a rich, savory flavor. Paired with the slightly anise-flavored, sweet tarragon and spicy chive in the white gravy, these biscuits are a refreshing twist on the classic.

THE RATIO This recipe has a 1:2 ratio of dough to filling.

1. Preheat oven to 425°F. Prepare biscuits as on page 28 but replace butter with duck fat. Bake as instructed.

2. While biscuits bake, make the gravy: melt butter in a large skillet over medium heat. Add onions and cook, stirring constantly, for about 8 minutes, until translucent. Reduce heat to low and add flour. Cook, stirring constantly, for 2 minutes so that the flour flavor cooks out.

3. Pour in milk while stirring. Increase heat to medium and bring mixture to a boil. Cook for 5 to 10 minutes, until thick. Remove from heat and add salt, pepper, tarragon, and chives.

4. Serve biscuits with warm gravy.

> **VARIATION**
>
> **BACON FAT BISCUITS** Using a different fat can dramatically affect the flavor of a biscuit. See for yourself: Substitute bacon fat for the duck fat and omit the chives and tarragon. This variation makes a more traditional biscuits and gravy dish.

YIELD: 6 biscuits

PREP TIME: 30 minutes

BAKE TIME: 12 minutes

1 pound Biscuit Dough (page 28), prepared as at left

3 ounces cold, chopped duck fat

2 ounces (4 tablespoons) unsalted butter

½ small white onion, sliced

1 ounce all-purpose flour

2 cups whole milk

2 teaspoons salt

1 teaspoon ground black pepper

2 teaspoons fresh tarragon, diced

2 teaspoons chives, thinly sliced

SCONE DOUGH is a chemically leavened dough similar to biscuit dough. Where these doughs differ is in texture: biscuit dough is made using cold butter, and heavy cream is responsible for giving scones their dense, crumbly texture. Use cream instead of milk in your scones. The cream's higher butterfat content imparts more buttery flavor than milk. The dough ratio is **8 FLOUR** : **2 SUGAR** : **6 LIQUID** .

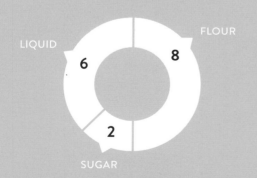

LIQUID
6

FLOUR
8

SUGAR
2

6	OUNCES BREAD FLOUR
2	OUNCES CAKE FLOUR
2	OUNCES SUGAR
6	FLUID OUNCES CREAM

Use this dough to make:
Sweet scones
Savory scones

SCONE DOUGH

| YIELD: 1 pound | PREP TIME: 10 minutes | BAKE TIME: 20–30 minutes |

6 ounces bread flour

2 ounces cake flour

2 ounces granulated sugar

4 teaspoons baking powder

½ teaspoon salt

Up to 6 ounces mix-ins
(optional; see page 43)

¾ cup heavy cream

MIXING THE DOUGH

Mix scone dough by hand or using a stand mixer.

By-Hand Method

1. Mix flours, sugar, baking powder, and salt in a large bowl. Stir in dry mix-ins (if using) until well combined.

2. Stir in heavy cream and wet mix-ins (if using) until dough begins to come together. It will be very thick.

Stand Mixer Method

1. Mix flours, sugar, baking powder, and salt with an electric stand mixer fitted with a paddle attachment on low speed until well combined.

2. Add dry mix-ins (if using) and mix on low speed until completely combined.

3. Pour in heavy cream and wet mix-ins (if using) and mix on medium-low speed until dough begins to come together.

SHAPING THE DOUGH

1. Position a rack in the center of the oven and preheat oven to 375°F. Transfer dough to a lightly floured surface and knead a few times with your hands until it holds its shape (see page 23 for kneading instructions).

2. Shape dough into a 4-by-8-inch rectangle with your hands. Cut rectangle in half to form two 4-inch squares. Cut each square diagonally to create four scones.

3. Arrange scones about an inch apart on a parchment paper–lined baking sheet.

4. Bake for 25 to 30 minutes, until golden.

Storage

Bake scones immediately, or store dough in an airtight container. Refrigerator: 2 days. Freezer: 1 month.

Qualities of Good Scone Dough

THE DOUGH: Scone dough should be slightly tacky and soft, making it very easy, albeit sticky, to manipulate. The dough should look rough.

THE PASTRY: Baked scones should be tender, crumbly, and slightly drier than biscuits. The outside crust should be firm, and the crumb inside should be softer and crumble easily.

FLOUR RATIO

Scone dough uses a 3:1 ratio of bread flour to cake flour—the opposite of biscuit dough's 1:3 ratio. This ratio develops more gluten, giving scone dough a firmer, chewier texture than biscuit dough. It also allows the dough to hold many more mix-ins while still retaining its shape.

ADDING SUGAR

Scone dough is the first of many doughs in this book to use sugar. While some require a small amount of sugar simply to feed yeast or to help brown the crust, in scone dough and others, more sugar is used to impart sweetness.

ADDING MIX-INS

Scone dough is very sturdy and made to be loaded up with mix-ins. You can add up to 6 ounces of dry mix-ins for every pound of dough and produce a delicious scone that will still hold its shape. Try chopped nuts, dried fruit, grated cheese, minced fresh herbs, grated citrus zest, or ground spices. Be careful when adding wet or juicy mix-ins like fresh fruit. If they break up during mixing, the extra moisture may cause the dough to spread during baking. You can also replace up to one-quarter of the cream in the recipe with another flavorful liquid, such as buttermilk, or add 1 teaspoon extract in addition to the cream.

SHAPING SCONE DOUGH

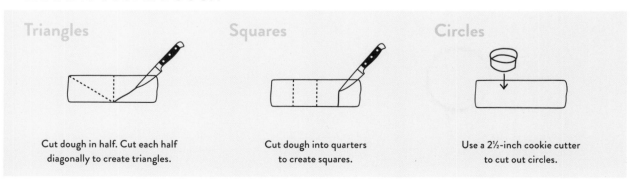

Triangles
Cut dough in half. Cut each half diagonally to create triangles.

Squares
Cut dough into quarters to create squares.

Circles
Use a 2½-inch cookie cutter to cut out circles.

SCONE DOUGH RECIPES

BROWN BUTTER BLUEBERRY SCONES

(2:1)

THE RECIPE Blueberry scones are one of my favorite pastries to pick up at any of the dozen bakeries I frequent around town. The sweet, dense dough dotted with juicy blueberries just can't be beat. They are also one of the easiest pastries to make.

THE RATIO Scones can handle a lot of mix-ins, and this recipe is the proof. It has a 2:1 ratio of dough to mix-ins.

1. Follow the instructions for mixing and shaping scone dough beginning on page 42, gently stirring in blueberries with dry ingredients with a wooden spoon.

2. Heat butter in a small saucepan over medium heat, stirring constantly, until it begins to turn light brown and has a nutty aroma. Brush brown butter over scones and sprinkle with brown sugar. Bake for about 25 minutes, until golden brown, and serve.

BROWN BUTTER

Brown butter, or *beurre noisette* (French for "hazelnut butter"), is the result of cooking butter until the milk solids separate from the butterfat. As the solids sink in the pan and continue to cook, they brown, creating the distinctive brown, or hazelnut, color. Before cooking, cut the butter into small pieces so that it melts evenly and quickly. Be sure to stir constantly to keep the butter from burning.

YIELD: 4 scones

PREP TIME: 20 minutes

BAKE TIME: 25 minutes

1 pound Scone Dough (page 42), prepared as at left

6 ounces fresh blueberries

2 ounces (4 tablespoons) unsalted butter

½ ounce light brown sugar

> VARIATION
>
> **DARK CHOCOLATE SCONES** Omit brown butter. Replace blueberries with 6 ounces chopped dark chocolate. Top scones with brown sugar and ½ ounce chocolate shavings.

CAPOCOLLO BRIE SCONES

16:5

THE RECIPE These savory scones are rich and boldly flavored with rosemary and capocollo. The brie, which melts into the dough as it cooks, adds a tangy creaminess. The result is an unforgettable addition to the dinner table.

THE RATIO This recipe has a 16:5 ratio of dough to mix-ins.

1. Follow the instructions for mixing and shaping scone dough beginning on page 42, gently stirring in capocollo, brie, and rosemary with the dry ingredients.

2. Brush tops of scones with melted butter, and sprinkle with salt.

3. Bake for about 25 to 30 minutes, until lightly golden, and serve.

CAPOCOLLO

Capocollo (sometimes found in stores as coppa, capicola, or gabagoul) is a dry-cured pork cut that runs from the head down to the shoulder. When ordering capocollo, ask the butcher to slice it very thin. If you have a preferred cured pork cut, feel free to try it in this recipe instead.

> **VARIATION**
>
> **BACON CHIVE SCONES** Replace the capocollo with chopped cooked bacon, the brie with parmesan, and the rosemary with diced chives.

YIELD: 4 scones

PREP TIME: 10 minutes

BAKE TIME: 30 minutes

1 pound Scone Dough (page 42), prepared as at left

2 ounces capocollo, thinly sliced

2 ounces brie, cut into ¼-inch cubes

2 teaspoons fresh rosemary, chopped

1 ounce (2 tablespoons) unsalted butter, melted

¼ teaspoon salt

PIE DOUGH is made using the biscuit-mixing method, in which butter is suspended in an unleavened dough rather than fully mixed in. Compared to biscuit dough, the chunks of fat in pie dough are larger and less liquid is used, resulting in a flaky, less tender crumb. Although this dough doesn't require the precision necessary for making puff pastry, it still has a flaky texture. It can be baked either in a pie dish or free-form. The dough ratio is **8 FLOUR : 7 FAT : 2 LIQUID** .

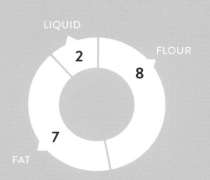

LIQUID
2
FLOUR
8
FAT
7

- 6 OUNCES BREAD FLOUR
- 2 OUNCES CAKE FLOUR
- 7 OUNCES BUTTER
- 2 FLUID OUNCES WATER

Use this dough to make:

Closed pies
Open-faced pies
Galettes
Hand pies
Pot pies
Crackers

PIE DOUGH

| YIELD: 1 pound | PREP TIME: 2 hours | BAKE TIME: varies |

6 ounces bread flour

2 ounces cake flour

1 teaspoon salt

7 ounces (14 tablespoons) unsalted butter, cold

¼ cup water

MIXING THE DOUGH

There are two ways to mix pie dough: by hand or using a food processor.

By-Hand Method

1. Mix flours and salt in a large bowl. Chop butter into ½-inch chunks and add to flour mixture. Pinch or cut butter into flour using your fingers or a pastry cutter, breaking it into pieces about the size of large peas. If using your hands, work quickly to keep butter from melting.

2. Pour water into flour mixture. Mix dough with your hands or about 10 to 15 turns of a wooden spoon, until it just starts to come together. The dough will be very tough and should remain in a few large chunks.

3. Place dough on a lightly floured surface and push chunks together. Knead 4 to 5 times, just until it holds together. Flatten dough into a disk about 1 inch thick. Wrap tightly in parchment paper and let rest in the refrigerator for at least 1 hour.

Food Processor Method

1. Pulse flours and salt in the bowl of a food processor 2 or 3 times to combine. Chop butter into ½-inch cubes and add to flour mixture. Pulse for 1 second about 8 times, until butter is in pieces about the size of large peas. Add water and pulse 3 to 4 times, until dough begins to come together. It may remain in a few large chunks.

2. Place dough on a lightly floured surface and push chunks together. Knead 4 to 5 times, until it holds its shape. Flatten dough into a disk about 1 inch thick. Wrap tightly in parchment paper and let rest in the refrigerator for at least 1 hour.

Storage

Because pie dough contains no chemical leavener, it stores well wrapped tightly in parchment paper. You can easily double, triple, or even quadruple this dough recipe and store enough for a month's worth of pies. If you know the shape of the dough you plan to roll later, form it into that shape, about 1 inch thick, before storing to make rolling it later easier. Refrigerator: 4 days. Freezer: 4 months.

Qualities of Good Pie Dough

THE DOUGH: Pie dough should be fairly dry and tough to manipulate. You should see dots of butter throughout the dough. When rolling, the dough should hold together well and not tear or break.

THE PASTRY: Once baked, pie crust should be very flaky. Crust that isn't in contact with filling should crumble and flake easily. Portions touching filling will be slightly less flaky but should still be dry and crisp.

FLOUR RATIO

This pie dough uses a 3:1 ratio of bread flour to cake flour. The large amount of bread flour results in a relatively high protein content, which helps create a flakier, crisper crust. You may also use all bread flour or all all-purpose flour.

ASSEMBLING THE PIE

1

Roll dough into a 14-inch circle.

2

Place dough in a 9-inch pie dish.

3

Trim excess dough from edges.

4

Pour filling into pie.

5

Top with any of the options on pages 52–53.

LATTICE TOP

1

Roll dough into a 10-inch circle.

2

Cut dough into 18 (½-inch) strips.
Discard the two outermost strips.

3

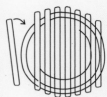

Arrange every other strip vertically
on top of the pie, spaced evenly.

4

Lift every other strip halfway. Lay a
long strip across the pie horizontally.

5

Fold strips down. Lift alternating strips.
Lay another horizontal strip down.

6

Repeat until pie is covered. Trim excess
dough and crimp edges tightly.

LEAF TOP

1

Roll dough into a 15-inch circle.

2

Cut out small leaf shapes with a
cookie cutter or paring knife.

3

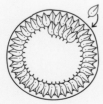

Arrange leaves in an overlapping
row starting at the edge.

4

Add another row of leaves,
overlapping slightly with the first.

5

Continue until the entire pie is covered.

CLOSED TOP

1

Roll dough into a 10-inch circle.

2

Place dough on top of pie.
Trim excess and seal edges tightly.

3

Cut steam vents into top of pie.

GALETTE

1

Roll dough into a 15-inch circle.

2

Pour filling onto the center, leaving 3
inches bare around the edges.

3

Fold over the edges, overlapping
folds as necessary.

HAND PIE

1

Roll dough into 6-inch circles.

2

Place filling on one half, leaving
½ inch bare around the edge.
Fold over other half.

3

Press edges together tightly and crimp.

FLUTED EDGE

1 Trim excess dough from edges.

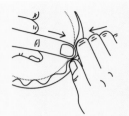

2 Place your thumb and first knuckle against outside of crust. Press dough between them, creating a crimp.

3 Repeat until entire edge is fluted.

BRAIDED EDGE

1 Trim around edge of dish, and roll excess dough into a 6-by-10-inch rectangle. Cut into 18 (¼-by-10-inch) strips.

2 Braid 3 strips together on the lip of the dish.

3 Crimp 3 more strips to the ends and continue braiding. Repeat until the entire edge is braided.

OTHER EDGES

Checkered

Cut a slit halfway into the edge every ¼ inch, creating tabs. Fold over every other tab, creating a checkered pattern.

Petal

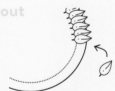

Press the edge of a spoon into dough as shown, making 3 semicircles. Repeat, leaving a small gap between petals.

Cutout

Cut out shapes with a cookie cutter or knife. Overlap shapes around edge, pressing gently to adhere.

Scalloped

Press your thumb or finger into edge of dough to create a dimple. Repeat, leaving a small gap between dimples.

Rope

Pinch dough gently with your thumb and first knuckle. Rock gently to the inside, creating a diagonal ridge. Repeat.

PIE DOUGH RECIPES

APPLE SPICE PIE

THE RECIPE Nothing is more classic than an apple pie, and sometimes you just can't improve upon a classic. This recipe is really your mother's—and her mother's—apple pie. I like to use Pink Lady apples because of their sweet and tart notes. For an even tarter pie, try Granny Smith.

THE RATIO Pies are proof that dough can handle heavy lifting. This recipe has a 1:3 ratio of dough to filling.

1. Position a rack in the center of the oven and preheat oven to 400°F. Divide prepared pie dough into 2 (1-inch-thick) disks, wrap tightly in parchment paper, and refrigerate. Heat butter in a large pot over medium-low heat. Add apples and cook, stirring occasionally, for about 5 minutes, until they begin to soften. Add sugars, lemon juice, cinnamon, nutmeg, allspice, ginger, and salt. Stir until evenly mixed. Cook for another 10 minutes, until apples are soft and juices begin to thicken.

2. Mix ½ cup water and cornstarch in a small bowl. Stir into apple mixture. Increase heat to medium-high and cook, stirring frequently, until filling comes to a boil and thickens. Cook, stirring constantly, for another 30 seconds. Set aside.

3. Place one dough disk on a lightly floured surface. Roll into a circle about 14 inches in diameter. Transfer dough to a 9-inch pie dish and press into the bottom of the dish, taking care not to let dough stretch. Lightly press dough down around the edges of the dish and cut off any excess. Pour in filling, creating a mound in the center. Set aside.

4. Place second disk of dough on a lightly floured surface. Roll into a circle about 14 inches in diameter and place on top of pie dish. Press edges to seal pie shut. Cut 4 tear-drop holes in the center of the pie to let steam escape during cooking. Cut excess dough from edges. Create a rope edge (see page 54). Lightly brush dough with egg wash. Bake for about 30 minutes, until crust is golden brown. Let cool on a wire rack before serving.

YIELD: 1 (9-inch) closed pie

PREP TIME: 30 minutes

BAKE TIME: 30 minutes

2 pounds prepared Pie Dough (double the recipe on page 50)

2 ounces (4 tablespoons) unsalted butter, room temperature

6 pounds Pink Lady apples, peeled, cored, and cut into 8 wedges each

3 ounces granulated sugar

3 ounces brown sugar

2 tablespoons lemon juice

2 teaspoons ground cinnamon

½ teaspoon ground nutmeg

¼ teaspoon ground allspice

¼ teaspoon ground ginger

1 teaspoon salt

1 ounce (¼ cup) cornstarch

1 egg, beaten (egg wash)

BOURBON CHOCOLATE PECAN PIE

1:2

THE RECIPE Although many people save pecan pie for the holidays, we Texans like a slice after every meal. So to make it stand out during the holidays, I serve this version. It's nutty, sweet, and chocolatey—chocolate is, after all, the only thing that can make pecan pie better. Bourbon and cinnamon add just a hint of spicy flavor.

THE RATIO This recipe has a 1:2 ratio of dough to filling.

1. Position a rack in the center of the oven and preheat oven to 375°F. Mix brown sugar and corn syrup in a large bowl. Add eggs one at a time, mixing well after each addition. Stir in bourbon, cinnamon, vanilla, and butter. Mix in chopped pecans and chocolate until well combined. Set aside.

2. Transfer dough from the refrigerator to a lightly floured surface. Roll into a circle about 14 inches in diameter. Transfer dough to a 9-inch pie dish and press into the bottom of the dish, taking care not to let it stretch. Lightly press dough down around the edges and cut off any excess.

3. Pour filling into pie. Arrange pecan halves around the edge, pressing down lightly so they stay in place. Bake for 40 to 45 minutes, until top is browned and filling is set. Let cool on a wire rack before serving.

Homemade Gourd Puree

You can make puree for pies from just about any type of gourd, including acorn squash, spaghetti squash, and pumpkin. Cut each gourd in half and remove seeds and innards. Place face up on a parchment paper–lined baking sheet and bake at 375°F until the flesh is soft, anywhere from 35 minutes for a small pie pumpkin to 1 hour for a large butternut squash. Scoop out the flesh and puree in a food processor until smooth. Yield: varies.

YIELD: 1 (9-inch) open-faced pie

PREP TIME: 20 minutes

BAKE TIME: 45 minutes

1 pound prepared Pie Dough (page 50), refrigerated

3 ounces brown sugar

4 fluid ounces (½ cup) light corn syrup

4 eggs

½ ounce (1 tablespoon) bourbon

½ teaspoon ground cinnamon

½ teaspoon vanilla extract

2 ounces (4 tablespoons) unsalted butter, melted

12 ounces pecans, roughly chopped

6 ounces dark (52%–70% cacao) chocolate, roughly chopped

Pecan halves, for decoration

PUMPKIN SQUASH PIE For another twist on a holiday classic, try this pumpkin and butternut squash pie. Use 1 pound Pie Dough (page 50) and prepare as at left. For the filling: Mix 2 eggs, 1½ cups pumpkin puree, ½ cup butternut squash puree (see Homemade Gourd Puree, at left), ¼ cup coconut milk, 1 teaspoon vanilla extract, 6 ounces brown sugar, ½ ounce (2 tablespoons) all-purpose flour, 2 teaspoons ground cinnamon, 1 teaspoon orange zest, and 1 teaspoon ground ginger in a large bowl until well combined. Pour into pie crust and bake at 375°F for about 1 hour, until filling is set.

PLUM CHERRY GALETTE

(1:3)

THE RECIPE A galette (or crostata) is a free-form pastry that can be made with pie dough, as here, or 1 pound of shortcrust dough (page 72) for a crumblier, less flaky version; either way, follow the instructions below. The dark plums and cherries are rich and tart; cinnamon and orange balance the tartness.

THE RATIO This recipe has a 1:3 ratio of dough to filling.

1. Place a baking stone in the very bottom of the oven. Preheat oven to 425°F. Roll dough into a circle about 15 inches in diameter and place it on a lightly floured, 16-inch square piece of parchment paper on top of a pizza peel or baking sheet.

2. Mix flours and sugar in a small bowl. Sprinkle mixture over dough, leaving 3 inches bare around the edge. Arrange plums and cherries on top. Fold edges of dough over fruit, overlapping it onto itself every couple of inches as necessary.

3. Mix orange zest, cinnamon, and salt in a small bowl. Lightly brush exposed pastry with egg wash. Sprinkle orange zest mixture over filling and dough.

4. Carefully slide galette and parchment paper off the pizza peel onto the hot baking stone in the oven. Bake for 20 minutes. Reduce oven temperature to 375°F and bake for another 25 to 35 minutes, until crust is golden brown. Use the pizza peel to transfer galette and parchment paper from baking stone to a wire rack, and let cool before serving. Top cooled galette with prosecco cream if desired.

TIP *If you don't have a baking stone and pizza peel, assemble the galette on a parchment paper–lined baking sheet. Bake on the bottom rack of the oven for the same amount of time.*

YIELD: 1 (10-inch) galette

PREP TIME: 30 minutes

BAKE TIME: 55 minutes

1 pound prepared Pie Dough (page 50), refrigerated

2 pounds Black Splendor plums or other tart plums, pitted and cut into 8 wedges each

1 pound Dark Hudson cherries or other sweet cherries, pitted and halved

½ ounce oat flour

¼ ounce tablespoon all-purpose flour

½ ounce granulated sugar

1 tablespoon orange zest

¼ teaspoon ground cinnamon

¼ teaspoon salt

1 egg, beaten (egg wash)

Prosecco Cream, optional (recipe at right)

Prosecco Cream

Combine 1 cup heavy cream and ¼ cup superfine sugar in a mixing bowl. Whip with an electric mixer on high speed until stiff peaks form. Reduce speed to medium and slowly pour in 2 tablespoons prosecco. Return to high speed and whip until stiff peaks form. Yield: 2 cups.

VARIATION

MINI BLUEBERRY PEACH GALETTES Divide dough in half and roll into 2 circles about 9 inches in diameter. Mix 1 ounce all-purpose flour, ½ ounce (3 ½ teaspoons) granulated sugar, and ½ teaspoon salt in a small bowl. Sprinkle half of it onto the center of each disk, leaving 2 inches bare around the edges. Divide 2 pounds sliced peaches and 1 pound blueberries between the two galettes, arranging them over the flour mixture. Fold edges of dough over filling. Brush galettes with egg wash and sprinkle ½ ounce (2 tablespoons) brown sugar and 1 teaspoon grated, peeled fresh ginger on each. Bake as at left.

BLUEBERRY MASCARPONE HAND PIES

THE RECIPE Hand pies may be baking's greatest contribution to society. What's better than a pie you can take with you?

THE RATIO This recipe has a 1:1 ratio of dough to filling, making it perfect for people who like pie crust as much as filling.

1. Position a rack in the center of the oven and preheat oven to 400°F. Divide prepared pie dough into 6 (½-inch-thick) disks, wrap tightly in parchment paper, and refrigerate. Puree half the blueberries in a food processor or blender. Transfer to a large pot and add remaining whole berries, 1 cup of the water, sugar, and lemon juice. Bring to a boil over high heat. Reduce heat slightly to maintain a boil and cook uncovered for 15 minutes, stirring occasionally, until filling begins to thicken.

2. Mix the remaining ¼ cup water and cornstarch in a small bowl. Add to blueberry mixture and stir. Return to a boil. Cook, stirring constantly, for another 30 seconds, until thick. Let cool slightly, and then add mascarpone, lemon zest, and salt. Stir until well combined and set aside.

3. Place dough disks on a lightly floured surface and roll each into a circle about 6 inches in diameter. Return all but one to the refrigerator.

4. Spoon about ¼ cup filling onto one half of the dough, leaving ½ inch bare around the edge. Fold the other half over filling and press edges together tightly to seal (see page 54 for edging options). Cut a few ½-inch slits in the top with a sharp knife to let steam escape during baking. Place hand pie on a parchment paper–lined baking sheet in the refrigerator. One at a time, repeat with the remaining 5 dough disks, adding to the baking sheet in the refrigerator as they are completed.

YIELD: 6 hand pies

PREP TIME: 30 minutes

BAKE TIME: 25 minutes

2 pounds prepared Pie Dough (double the recipe on page 50)

1½ pounds fresh blueberries, divided

1¼ cups water, divided

12 ounces granulated sugar

2 tablespoons lemon juice

2 ounces (½ cup) cornstarch

6 ounces mascarpone

2 tablespoons lemon zest (from 1–2 large or 2–3 small lemons)

2 teaspoons salt

1 egg, beaten (egg wash)

1 ounce brown sugar

5. Brush unbaked pies with egg wash and top with brown sugar. Bake for 20 to 25 minutes, until crust is golden brown. Let cool on the pan slightly before transferring to a wire cooling rack, and let cool completely before serving.

VARIATIONS

CLASSIC CHERRY HAND PIES Bring 1 pound pitted and halved fresh cherries, 1 cup water, 10 ounces granulated sugar, and 2 tablespoons lemon juice to a boil in a large pot. Reduce heat slightly to maintain a boil and cook for 10 minutes. Mix 2 ounces (½ cup) cornstarch and ¼ cup water in a small bowl. Add to filling and stir. Return to a boil, cooking for another 30 seconds, until thick. Proceed with step 3 of recipe.

CHOCOLATE HAZELNUT HAND PIES Mix 1 pound hazelnut chocolate spread, ½ cup freshly brewed hot coffee, ¼ cup heavy cream, 6 ounces chopped roasted hazelnuts, and 2 tablespoons orange zest in a bowl. Proceed with step 3 of recipe.

GRILLED CORN AND THYME CHICKEN POT PIES

(1:8)

THE RECIPE Chicken pot pie is as comforting a recipe as they come. Mine uses two of my favorite summer ingredients: corn and thyme. Grilling the corn and chicken gives both a delicious charred flavor.

THE RATIO This recipe has a 1:8 ratio of dough to filling.

1. Shape prepared pie dough into a 1-inch-thick disk, wrap tightly in parchment paper, and refrigerate. Prepare grill for chicken and corn. For a charcoal grill: Light charcoal. Let coals ash over, about 20 to 30 minutes. Push coals to one half of the grill and spread in an even layer, leaving the other half free of coals. Place the grate over the coals to heat it. For a propane grill: Turn one side of the grill to high and the other to low.

2. Place chicken skin side down on the hot side of the grill. Cook for 3 to 5 minutes, until lightly browned. Flip chicken and cook for another 3 to 5 minutes, until the other side is lightly browned. Move chicken to the cooler side of the grill, skin side down. Place corn on the grill. Cover and cook for about 30 to 35 minutes, until the chicken juices run clear and the internal temperature of the meat is 165°F.

3. Meanwhile, melt butter in a large saucepan over medium heat. Add fennel, onions, and thyme and cook for about 10 minutes, until onions are soft and translucent. Add garlic and cook for another 2 minutes. Reduce heat to low and add flour. Cook, stirring constantly, for 2 minutes so that the flavor of the flour cooks out. Add stock, cream, potatoes, and bay leaf. Bring to a simmer over medium-high heat. Reduce heat to maintain a slow simmer. Cook uncovered for 30 minutes.

4. Preheat oven to 350°F. Cut corn kernels off the cob and dice or shred chicken. Add corn and chicken to sauce. Remove and discard bay leaf. Divide filling among four baking dishes.

YIELD: 4 (2-cup) pot pies

PREP TIME: 1 hour

COOK TIME: 30 minutes

1 pound prepared Pie Dough (page 50)

2 pounds uncooked bone-in chicken breast

2 ears corn, shucked

4 tablespoons unsalted butter

½ bulb fennel, sliced

½ yellow onion, sliced

1 tablespoon chopped fresh thyme

2 garlic cloves, diced

2 tablespoons all-purpose flour

3½ cups chicken stock

½ cup heavy cream

1 large yellow potato, diced

1 bay leaf

1 egg, beaten (egg wash)

5. Roll pie dough into a 12-inch square and cut four squares large enough to cover each baking dish. Top each dish with one square, brush dough with egg wash, and sprinkle with salt. Cut a slit in the center of each to let the steam escape. Bake for 25 to 30 minutes, until crust is golden brown and filling is bubbly, and serve.

ROASTED CHICKEN POT PIE

If you don't have a grill, or it is too cold to venture outside, you can roast the chicken in the oven at 375°F for 45 to 55 minutes, until the juices run clear. In the final 30 minutes of roasting, add corn cobs, in their husks.

> ### VARIATION
>
> **AUTUMN VEGETABLE POT PIES** Omit grilled chicken, corn, fennel, and thyme. Add ½ cup peeled and diced parsnips and 1 tablespoon diced fresh rosemary with the onions. Add 2 cups cubed butternut squash, 2 cups cubed yams, and 1 cup cubed pumpkin with the potatoes. Replace chicken stock with vegetable stock.

ORANGE COOKIE CRUMB CRUST

Although a cookie-crumb pie crust is not a true dough, we can't talk about pies without mentioning it. Simply a mixture of pulverized cookies, butter, sugar, and salt, it's easy to make, popular, and, best of all, delicious. You can use store-bought graham crackers or any dry biscuit-style cookie ground finely. Here are two versions made using Sweetcrust Dough (page 88), the same dough used for many sweet tarts. This "dough" can be used as the base for lemon meringue pies, chocolate pudding pies, cream pies, custard pies, and more.

YIELD: 1½ pounds

PREP TIME: 10 minutes

BAKE TIME: 25 minutes

1 pound Pâte Sucrée à l'Orange Cookies (page 89)

8 ounces granulated sugar

4 ounces (8 tablespoons) unsalted butter, melted

½ teaspoon salt

1. Preheat oven to 375°F. Puree cookies in a food processor until they are uniformly fine crumbs. Mix crumbs, sugar, melted butter, and salt in a large bowl with a spoon or your hands. The mixture will be slightly dry and crumbly.

2. Firmly press mixture into the bottom and up the sides of a pie dish. Bake for 20 to 25 minutes, until edges begin to brown and crust is set. Let cool completely before filling and serving.

VARIATION

CHOCOLATE COOKIE CRUMBLES CRUST Substitute 1 pound Pâte Sucrée au Chocolat Cookies (page 89) for the orange cookies.

TIP *You also can make mini pies with cookie crusts: divide crumb mixture equally among 4 mini (6-inch) pie dishes before baking.*

Storage

This faux pie dough should be baked right away. Allow baked shell to cool completely before adding cold fillings such as custards or mousses.

ORANGE CREAMSICLE PIES

1:5

THE RECIPE Growing up, creamsicles were one of my favorite desserts. With this recipe I turned my beloved childhood confection into a pie using a cookie crumb crust. Although not a true pastry dough, it's worth breaking the rules for.

THE RATIO This recipe has a 1:5 ratio of dough to filling.

1. Place orange peels in a medium pot, cover with cold water, and bring to a boil over high heat. Immediately remove from heat, and drain and discard water. Repeat 3 more times to remove the bitterness from the peels, and then pat peels dry with a paper towel.

2. Place peels and milk in a medium pot. Cut vanilla bean in half lengthwise. Scrape seeds out of the pod with the tip of a paring knife. Add seeds and pod to milk. Heat milk over medium heat until it reaches the scalding point (180°F on a clipped-on thermometer); it will begin to steam and appear slightly foamy. Remove from heat and let steep, covered, for 1 hour.

3. Remove peels and vanilla bean pod. Heat milk over medium heat until it returns to the scalding point. Meanwhile, mix cornstarch, sugar, salt, eggs, and orange zest in a large bowl. Once milk is scalded, temper the egg mixture: slowly pour a third of the milk into egg mixture, stirring constantly. Pour tempered egg mixture back into pot. Bring to a boil over medium heat, stirring frequently, until boiling and thick. Cook for another 30 seconds, stirring constantly. Let cool completely.

4. Fill pie crusts with orange cream. Top with dollops of whipped cream or pipe whipped cream over the tops, and serve.

continued on next page

YIELD: 4 (6-inch) mini pies

PREP TIME: 3 hours

BAKE TIME: None

1½ pounds Orange Cookie Crumb Crust, mixed as on page 66, baked in 4 (6-inch) pie dishes, and completely cooled

2 cups orange peels (from about 6 oranges)

1½ quarts whole milk

1 vanilla bean

3 ounces (¾ cup) cornstarch

12 ounces granulated sugar

1 teaspoon salt

4 eggs

1 tablespoon orange zest

1 quart Vanilla Whipped Cream, cold (page 69)

For a distinctive look, pipe a different pattern on each pie (as in the photo, opposite). Fit four pastry bags with four different large piping tips. Fill bags with whipped cream and twist shut. Grasp the twisted portion between the thumb and pointer finger of your dominant hand, and use your other hand to hold and guide the tip. Place the tip about 1 inch from the top of the pie, perpendicular to the pie. Squeeze quickly with your dominant hand, holding the tip in place with your other hand, to create a little ball of frosting. Stop squeezing and quickly lift the tip. Repeat until pie is covered.

Vanilla Whipped Cream

Whip 2 cups very cold heavy cream with an electric mixer on high speed until it forms soft peaks. Reduce speed to medium-high and slowly add 2 ounces ($\frac{1}{4}$ cup) granulated sugar. Increase speed to high and whip to stiff peaks. Add $\frac{1}{2}$ teaspoon vanilla extract and whip for another few seconds to incorporate. Refrigerate until ready to serve. Yield: 1 quart.

VARIATIONS

BANANA BRÛLÉE PIE Omit whipped cream. Top pies with sliced bananas, cut on the bias. Sprinkle 1 ounce granulated sugar over each pie. Heat sugar with the flame of a propane kitchen torch until it caramelizes.

MILK CHOCOLATE MOUSSE PIE Replace crust with a Chocolate Cookie Crumbles Crust (page 66). Replace orange cream with Milk Chocolate Mousse (below).

Milk Chocolate Mousse

Whip 1 cup heavy cream and $\frac{1}{2}$ teaspoon vanilla extract with an electric mixer on high speed until soft peaks form. Refrigerate. Heat $1\frac{1}{2}$ ounces honey just to the boiling point (212°F). Meanwhile, whip 2 egg yolks until they are thick and form ribbons. Whisk warm honey into egg yolks. Continue whipping until mixture has cooled and is thick. Melt 6 ounces dark chocolate in a bowl over a large pot of simmering water. Whisk chocolate into egg mixture and whip until blended. Fold in whipped cream. Yield: About 1 quart.

SHORTCRUST DOUGH is an unsweetened, unleavened dough used to make tarts, pies, and cookies; it goes by several French names, including *pâte brisée* (meaning "broken dough"), *pâte à foncer* ("darkened dough"), and *pâte sablée* ("sandy dough"). Unlike pie dough, whose texture depends on cold butter, shortcrust is made with room-temperature butter that is more fully mixed in, creating a crumbly texture. The dough ratio is

8 FLOUR : **4½ FAT** : **1¾ EGG** .

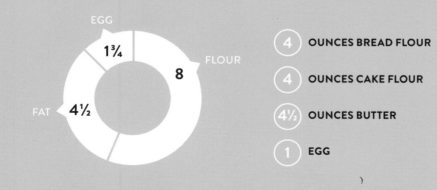

EGG 1¾

FLOUR 8

FAT 4½

4 OUNCES BREAD FLOUR

4 OUNCES CAKE FLOUR

4½ OUNCES BUTTER

1 EGG

Use this dough to make:

Sweet tarts

Savory tarts

Tartlets

Mini tart cups

Pop tarts

Cookies

SHORTCRUST DOUGH

| YIELD: 1 pound | PREP TIME: 20 minutes | BAKE TIME: 40 minutes |

4 ounces bread flour

4 ounces cake flour

½ teaspoon salt

4½ ounces (9 tablespoons) unsalted butter, room temperature

1 egg

MIXING THE DOUGH

Mix shortcrust dough by hand or using a stand mixer.

By-Hand Method

1. Mix flours and salt in a large bowl. Cut butter into ½-inch pieces and add to bowl. Pinch butter into flour mixture with your hands until mixture resembles coarse sand. Add egg and stir with a spoon until dough begins to come together. It may remain in a few large chunks with many smaller chunks.

2. Transfer dough to a lightly floured surface and lightly knead a few times, just until dough holds its shape. With your hands shape into a flat disk about 1 inch thick. Wrap tightly in parchment paper and refrigerate for about 1 hour, until firm.

Stand Mixer Method

1. In the large bowl of a stand mixer, mix flours and salt on low speed with a paddle attachment for a few seconds. Cut butter into ½-inch pieces and add to bowl. Mix on medium-low speed until butter is broken into tiny chunks and mixture resembles coarse sand. Add egg and mix on medium-low speed until dough begins to come together. It may remain in large chunks.

2. Transfer dough to a lightly floured surface and push together. Lightly knead a few times, just until dough holds its shape. With your hands shape dough into a flat disk about 1 inch thick. Wrap tightly in parchment paper and refrigerate for about 1 hour, until firm.

Storage

Shortcrust dough should be stored tightly wrapped in parchment paper. Refrigerator: 4 days. Freezer: 1 month. Store baked shortcrust dough in an airtight container at room temperature for up to 3 days.

Qualities of a Good Shortcrust

THE DOUGH: Shortcrust dough should be smooth, fairly soft, and easy to manipulate. Few if any specks of butter should be visible. The dough should hold together fairly well when rolled and tear or break only minimally.

THE PASTRY: Shortcrust, once baked, should be firm, crumbly, and easy to break into pieces.

BLIND BAKING

Unlike pie crusts, which are baked after being filled, short- and sweetcrust doughs require a preparation step called blind baking before a filling is added. A substitute weight, such as dried beans or pie weights, fills the empty crust to hold its shape during baking, and then the baked, cooled crust is loaded up with prepared or cold fillings. Turn the page for instructions.

Working with Shortcrust Dough

Shortcrust dough is soft thanks to its high fat content and the presence of egg. Refrigerating it makes it firm enough to roll and allows the gluten time to rest, which makes the dough easier to work with.

After mixing the dough but before refrigerating it, form it into roughly the shape you'll want it in when you prepare to bake it, and flatten it as much as possible (ideally about 1 inch thick), both to reduce the time spent rolling it later and to speed up the chill time.

A chilled marble slab is the ideal work surface for shortcrust dough, because it keeps the dough cool and helps prevents sticking. Chill the slab in the freezer for 30 minutes before rolling the dough.

Work quickly when rolling, or the shortcrust will become too soft and stick. Rotating the dough or carefully flipping it occasionally will help prevent sticking. If necessary, dusting flour on the work surface and rolling pin will help, but use as little as possible.

BLIND BAKING

1

Press dough into tart pan.
Trim excess with a paring knife.

2

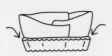

Line inside of crust with aluminum foil,
pressing it firmly in place. Leave excess
foil sticking up from the sides.

3

Fill foil-lined shell with pie weights or
dried beans such as pinto beans.

4 12–18 min

Blind bake according to recipe,
or until edges are lightly browned.

5

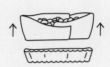

Carefully lift and remove foil sheet
and pie weights or dried beans,
leaving tart shell bare.

6

Poke holes in bottom of shell
with a fork or toothpick.

7 12–18 min

Bake uncovered according to recipe,
or until tart center is lightly golden.

SHORTCRUST DOUGH RECIPES

STRAWBERRY BAKEWELL TART

1:2

THE RECIPE I first tasted this classic English dessert, a cake-topped tart filled with Concord grape jelly, while working as an assistant pastry cook in Rebecca Masson's pastry shop, Fluff Bake Bar. I knew I would like it even before I tasted a bite. Here a sweet strawberry jam is layered under the moist cinnamon-flavored lemon almond cake.

THE RATIO This dessert is more filling than shortcrust, with a 1:2 ratio of dough to toppings.

1. Preheat oven to 375°F. Roll shortcrust dough into a 12-inch square on a lightly floured surface with a rolling pin. Carefully push dough into an 9-inch square tart pan with a removable bottom. Fold excess dough down into the pan to create thicker sides, or trim it to create a level top. Line dough with aluminum foil and fill with pie weights or dried beans. Blind bake (see pages 73–74) for 10 to 12 minutes, until sides are set. Remove foil and pie weights. Poke holes in bottom of dough with a toothpick or fork and bake for another 12 to 15 minutes, until crust is a light golden color. Set aside to cool; keep tart shell in tart pan.

2. Reduce oven temperature to 325°F. Meanwhile, prepare cake batter: Mix flours, baking powder, cinnamon, lemon zest, and salt in a large bowl; set aside. In the bowl of a stand mixer fitted with the paddle attachment, cream butter and sugar on medium-high speed until light and fluffy. Add eggs, one at a time, and mix well after each addition. Mix in vanilla. Add half of the flour mixture and mix on low speed until incorporated. Add milk and mix until incorporated. Add remaining flour mixture and mix until well combined. Scrape down the sides of the bowl as necessary.

3. Spread jam evenly over cooled crust. Pour cake batter over jam and carefully spread in an even layer all the way to the edges, ensuring no gaps are visible between the crust and batter.

4. Bake tart in the center of the oven for 35 to 40 minutes, until cake is set and does not jiggle. Cool completely before serving.

YIELD: 1 (9-inch) square tart

PREP TIME: 2 hours

BAKE TIME: 40 minutes

1 pound prepared Shortcrust Dough (page 72)

2 ounces almond flour

4 ounces bread flour

2 teaspoons baking powder

1 teaspoon ground cinnamon

2 tablespoons lemon zest

½ teaspoon salt

4 ounces (8 tablespoons) unsalted butter, room temperature

6 ounces granulated sugar

3 eggs

1 teaspoon vanilla extract

¼ cup whole milk

8 ounces Homemade Strawberry Jam (recipe at right)

Homemade Strawberry Jam

Heat 6 ounces fresh strawberries, 6 ounces granulated sugar, and 1 tablespoon lemon juice in a heavy-bottomed pot over high heat. Blend with an immersion blender. (Alternatively, blend ingredients in a blender before heating.) Bring mixture to a boil. Reduce heat to medium-high, or high enough to maintain a boil, and boil for about 10 minutes, until mixture is thick and jamlike. To test consistency, spoon a small amount onto a plate and place in the freezer for 2 minutes, until it cools to at least room temperature. If it's thick, the jam is done. If it's still runny, return mixture to a boil over medium-high heat and cook for another 2 minutes, until thick. Let cool completely before using. Yield: 8 ounces.

GRAPE JAM TARTLETS WITH SALTED LEMON CRÈME FRAÎCHE

2:3

THE RECIPE Even though I prefer strawberry jam in my bakewell tarts (page 76), I love grape jelly. Its pungent, sweet notes stand well on their own and pair wonderfully with many flavors. In these tartlets, salted lemon crème fraîche cuts the grapes' sweetness, and the buttery crust adds a nice bite and smooth flavor.

THE RATIO This is another example of how a tart shell can hold a lot of filling, with a 2:3 ratio of dough to filling.

1. Preheat oven to 375°F. Place shortcrust dough on a lightly floured surface and roll to ⅛ inch thick with a rolling pin. Cut out 3 (6-inch) circles with a cookie cutter and set aside. Combine scraps and roll them again. Cut out a fourth 6-inch circle.

2. Carefully push dough circles into 4 (4-inch) tart pans with removable bottoms. Fold excess dough back down into the pans to create thicker sides, or trim to create level tops. Line dough with aluminum foil and fill with pie weights or dried beans. Blind bake (see pages 73–74) for 10 to 12 minutes, until sides are set. Remove foil and pie weights. Poke holes in bottom of dough with a toothpick or fork and bake for another 12 to 15 minutes, until crust is a light golden color. Set aside to cool. Once cool, remove tart shells from pans.

3. Assemble tarts: Fill each with jelly and top with a dollop of crème fraîche. Sprinkle with lemon zest and salt, and serve.

YIELD: 4 (6-inch) tartlets

PREP TIME: 1 hour

BAKE TIME: 30 minutes

1 pound prepared Shortcrust Dough (page 72)

16 ounces Grape Jelly (recipe at right)

1 cup Crème Fraîche (recipe at right)

1 teaspoon lemon zest

1 teaspoon salt

VARIATION

TORCHED VANILLA TARTLETS Fill each tart shell with Vanilla Bean Pastry Cream (page 148). Sprinkle ½ ounce (3½ teaspoons) granulated sugar over each. Heat with a propane kitchen torch or place under a broiler until sugar caramelizes and hardens. Serve immediately.

Grape Jelly

Blend 1 pound halved, skin-on black grapes in a blender on high speed until completely pureed. Transfer to a large, heavy-bottomed pot with 8 ounces granulated sugar and 1 tablespoon lemon juice. Bring mixture to a boil, covered, over medium heat, and cook for 25 to 35 minutes, until thick enough to coat a spoon. Pour into a jar and let cool completely in the refrigerator. Yield: 16 ounces.

Crème Fraîche

Mix 1 tablespoon lemon juice into 1 cup heavy cream in a small bowl. Leave out, covered, at room temperature for 24 hours, stirring once after 8 to 12 hours. Yield: 8 ounces.

LEMON TEA MINI TARTS WITH A CHERRY ON TOP

1:3

THE RECIPE   I love tea and the unique flavor it can bring to a dish. Here, I've paired black tea–infused custard with lemon whipped cream, a couple tart cherries, and a sweet drizzle of honey. I only wish I could make my morning tea taste so good.

THE RATIO   This recipe has a 1:3 ratio of dough to filling.

1. Preheat oven to 375°F. On a lightly floured surface roll short-crust dough to ⅛ inch thick with a rolling pin. Cut out 8 (4-inch) circles with a cookie cutter. Carefully push each circle into a 2-inch tart pan with a removable bottom. Fold excess dough back down into pan, or trim.

2. Line dough with aluminum foil and fill with pie weights or dried beans. Blind bake (see pages 73–74) for 10 to 12 minutes, until sides are set. Remove foil and pie weights. Poke holes in bottom of dough with a toothpick or fork and bake for 12 to 15 minutes, until crust is light golden. Once cool, remove shells from pans.

3. Fill each shell with pastry cream. Top with whipped cream, a couple of cherries, and a drizzle of honey. Serve.

YIELD: 8 (2-inch) mini tarts

PREP TIME: 2 hours

BAKE TIME: 30 minutes

1 pound prepared Shortcrust Dough (page 72)

½ quart Oolong Tea Pastry Cream (recipe below)

½ quart Lemon-Infused Whipped Cream (recipe at right)

16 fresh dark cherries

½ ounce (2 teaspoons) honey

Oolong Tea Pastry Cream

Pour 2 cups milk into a medium saucepan. Cut 1 vanilla bean in half. Scrape seeds out of the pod with the tip of a paring knife. Add seeds and pod to milk. Tie ½ ounce loose oolong tea leaves in cheese cloth and add to milk. Heat over medium-high heat until milk reaches the scalding point (180°F on a clipped-on thermometer). Remove from heat and let steep, covered, for at least 20 minutes. Remove vanilla bean pod and tea. Return pan to medium heat until it reaches the scalding point again.

Meanwhile, mix ½ ounce (2 tablespoons) cornstarch, 2 ounces granulated sugar, ¼ teaspoon salt, and 1 egg in a large bowl. Temper egg mixture by slowly pouring a third of the hot milk into it, whisking constantly. Pour it back into the pot with remaining milk and heat over medium heat. Cook, stirring constantly, until pastry cream reaches a boil. Cook, stirring, for another 30 seconds. Remove from heat and stir in 2 ounces (4 tablespoons) unsalted butter. Cover with parchment paper and let cool completely in the refrigerator, about 1 hour. Yield: About ½ quart.

Lemon-Infused Whipped Cream

Cover 1 ounce lemon peels (from about 1 lemon) with cold water in a small saucepan. Bring to a boil. Strain. Refill saucepan with cold water and repeat 3 times. Dry lemon peels thoroughly with paper towels.

Place ½ cup heavy whipping cream and lemon peels in a small saucepan. Heat cream over medium-high heat until it reaches the scalding point (180°F on a clipped-on thermometer). Remove from heat and let steep, covered, for 20 minutes. Once at room temperature, place in the refrigerator to chill completely, at least 1 hour.

Pour cold cream through a sieve into the bowl of an electric stand mixer. Whip on high speed until it begins to thicken. Slowly pour in 1 ounce granulated sugar and continue to whip until stiff peaks form. Store in the refrigerator. Yield: About ½ quart.

HOMEMADE POP TARTS

(3:1)

THE RECIPE I have been obsessed with pop tarts since I was a kid. Making them at home may require a little extra work, but the results are worth it. You can use nearly any filling recipe in this book, and four of my favorites follow this recipe. Each filling recipe makes enough for 9 pop tarts, but all can easily be scaled up or down.

THE RATIO With a 3:1 ratio of dough to filling, these pop tarts demonstrate how the combination of a little filling and a lot of dough can pack a lot of flavor.

1. Preheat oven to 375°F. Divide shortcrust dough into 2 equal portions. Shape each into a rectangle about 1 inch thick and refrigerate until firm. On a lightly floured surface roll each piece into a 12-by-9-inch rectangle about ¼ inch thick.

2. With a paring knife make a partial cut every 4 inches along the long sides of one piece of dough. Do the same every 3 inches along the short sides. Connect the lines using the knife to make a grid of 9 rectangles, and then cut along the lines to make 9 (3-by-4-inch) rectangles. Arrange rectangles on a parchment paper–lined baking sheet about ½ inch apart. Repeat with the second piece of dough.

3. Top 9 rectangles with about 1 ounce filling, leaving ½ inch bare around the edges. Brush edges with egg wash and top with the 9 remaining rectangles. With your fingertips press edges together tightly to seal, and then press edges with the tines of a fork to seal further. You can use a paring knife or pastry cutter to trim each tart so that the edges are straight. With a toothpick, poke 8 small holes in the top of each to allow steam to escape. Brush tarts with egg wash.

4. Bake for 15 to 20 minutes, until pop tarts are golden brown. If icing, let cool for a few minutes and then cover pop tarts with Sprinkle Icing. Serve.

YIELD: 9 pop tarts

PREP TIME: 1 hour

BAKE TIME: 20 minutes

2 pounds prepared Shortcrust Dough (double the recipe on page 72)

8 ounces filling of your choice (recipes at right, or use any of the fillings in this book)

1 egg, beaten (egg wash)

8 ounces Sprinkle Icing (recipe at right), optional

Unbaked pop tarts can be frozen in an airtight container for up to 1 month. Store baked pop tarts for up to 4 days in an airtight container at room temperature. Pop tarts without icing can be warmed in a toaster; before toasting, ensure pop tart is sealed shut completely.

Cinnamon Brown Sugar Filling

Mix 6 ounces light brown sugar, 2 teaspoons ground cinnamon, 1 ounce all-purpose flour, and ¼ teaspoon salt in a medium bowl. Yield: 8 ounces.

Strawberry Filling

This pairs well with Sprinkle Icing. Mix 7 ounces strawberry jam (such as on page 77) or the jam of your choice and 1 ounce (¼ cup) cornstarch until well combined. Yield: 8 ounces.

Chocolate Hazelnut Filling

Finely grind 3 ounces hazelnuts in a food processor. Melt 3 ounces milk chocolate in a bowl over a large pot of simmering water. Remove from heat and mix in hazelnuts, ¼ cup heavy cream, and ¼ teaspoon salt until well combined. Yield: 8 ounces.

S'Mores Filling

Top dough rectangles with 6 ounces Marshmallow Filling (page 97) followed by 2 ounces chopped milk chocolate. Yield: 8 ounces.

Sprinkle Icing

Mix 8 ounces powdered sugar, ½ teaspoon egg white, 1 tablespoon whole milk, and ½ teaspoon vanilla extract in a bowl. Spread icing over pop tarts while they are still warm but not hot. Drop 1 cup assorted-color sprinkles on top before icing sets. Yield: 8 ounces.

ROOT VEGETABLE SPIRAL TART

(1:2)

THE RECIPE Assembling this eye-catching tart requires a bit of finesse, but the delicious tangy and sweet flavors of carrots, parsnips, and rutabaga are too perfect to pass up. Spiraling thinly sliced vegetables close together allows them to cook evenly without losing their shape or texture. A little cream and nutmeg add a spicy, rich touch.

THE RATIO This recipe has a ratio of 1:2 of dough to filling.

1. Preheat oven to 375°F. On a lightly floured surface roll prepared shortcrust dough with a rolling pin into a 12-inch circle about ⅛ inch thick. Carefully press into a 9-inch round tart pan with a removable bottom. Fold excess dough back down into pan to create thicker sides, or trim to create a level top. Line dough with aluminum foil and fill with pie weights or dried beans. Blind bake (see pages 73–74) for 10 to 12 minutes, until sides are set. Remove foil and pie weights. Poke holes in bottom of dough with a toothpick or fork and bake for another 12 to 15 minutes, until crust is a light golden color. Set aside to cool; keep tart shell in the tart pan.

2. With a sharp knife trim any round edges from vegetables and cut into 1-by-1-inch strips (like large french fries). Slice each strip into 16 (1/16-inch-thick) strips with a mandoline slicer or a sharp chef's knife.

3. Arrange vegetable strips in a spiral, starting around the outside, placing them along the curve of the tart's sides, and alternating vegetables. As you fill the tart, ensure that the strips are pressed tightly against one another and the sides of the crust.

4. Mix heavy cream and nutmeg in a small bowl and pour over vegetables. Drizzle tart with olive oil and sprinkle with salt and pepper.

5. Bake in the center of the oven for about 60 minutes, until vegetables are just beginning to brown on top. Serve warm.

YIELD: 1 (9-inch) tart

PREP TIME: 1 hour

BAKE TIME: 60 minutes

1 pound prepared Shortcrust Dough (page 72)

1 pound carrots

12 ounces parsnips

12 ounces rutabaga

½ cup heavy cream

1 teaspoon grated nutmeg

Olive oil, to taste

Salt and pepper, to taste

SWEETCRUST DOUGH, often referred to as *pâte sucrée* (French for "sweetened dough"), is shortcrust's sister dough. The former contains sugar, as its name suggests, as well as less butter and a higher ratio of cake flour to bread flour, giving it a softer texture than that of shortcrust. Because the two recipes are so similar, you can substitute sweetcrust dough in any recipe that calls for shortcrust and vice versa. The dough ratio is **8 FLOUR** : **4 SUGAR** : **4 FAT** : **1¾ EGG** .

EGG
1¾
FLOUR
8
FAT
4
4
SUGAR

6 OUNCES CAKE FLOUR

2 OUNCES BREAD FLOUR

4 OUNCES SUGAR

4 OUNCES BUTTER

1 EGG

Use this dough to make:

Cookies

Tarts

Moon pies

Crumb crusts

SWEETCRUST DOUGH

| YIELD: 1 pound | PREP TIME: 1 hour | BAKE TIME: varies |

6 ounces cake flour

2 ounces bread flour

4 ounces granulated sugar

½ teaspoon salt

4 ounces (8 tablespoons) unsalted butter

1 egg

MIXING THE DOUGH

Mix sweetcrust dough by hand or using a stand mixer.

By-Hand Method

1. Mix flours, sugar, and salt in a large bowl. Cut butter into ½-inch pieces and add to flour mixture. Pinch butter into flour mixture with your hands until mixture resembles coarse sand. Add egg and stir with a spoon until dough begins to come together. It may contain a few large chunks.

2. Transfer to a lightly floured surface and push together. Lightly knead a few times, just until dough holds its shape. Shape with your hands into a flat disk about 1 inch thick. Wrap tightly in parchment paper and refrigerate for about 1 hour, until firm.

Stand Mixer Method

1. In the large bowl of an electric stand mixer, mix flours, sugar, and salt with the paddle attachment on low speed for a few seconds. Cut butter into ½-inch pieces and add to bowl. Mix on medium-low speed until mixture resembles coarse sand. Add egg and mix on medium-low speed until dough begins to come together. It may remain in a few large chunks.

2. Transfer to a lightly floured surface and push dough together. Lightly knead a few times, just until dough holds its shape. Shape into a flat disk about 1 inch thick. Wrap tightly in parchment paper and refrigerate for 1 hour, until firm.

Storage

Sweetcrust dough, like shortcrust dough, can be stored tightly wrapped in parchment paper. Refrigerator: 4 days. Freezer: 1 month. Store finished baked goods in an airtight container at room temperature for up to 4 days.

Qualities of a Good Sweetcrust

THE DOUGH: Sweetcrust dough will be very soft and grainy and will break easily. It is very easy to manipulate but becomes difficult to roll and move if it gets too warm.

THE PASTRY: Baked sweetcrust will be dry, crumbly, and firmer than shortcrust dough.

Working with Sweetcrust Dough

Sweetcrust shares the characteristics of shortcrust dough that make the latter soft. Adding sugar makes it even softer and slightly more challenging to work with. See "Working with Shortcrust Dough," page 73, for tips.

If shortcrust dough breaks while you're rolling it or placing it in a pan, don't be afraid to push it back together or to use a little extra dough to fill in a crack. In fact, sweetcrust dough is so soft and malleable that you could skip rolling it and press the just-mixed dough into a pan, although I recommend rolling it according to the recipe.

CHILL THE SURFACE

A marble slab that has been chilled for 30 minutes is an ideal surface for rolling sweetcrust dough; the chill will help keep the dough from sticking.

MAKING SWEETCRUST SUGAR COOKIES

Sweetcrust dough is very similar to sugar cookie dough, though sugar cookies tend to have a cakier texture because they contain less flour. Preheat oven to 375°F. On a lightly floured surface roll prepared sweetcrust dough to ¼ inch thick. Cut out cookies with a 2-inch cookie cutter. Knead leftover dough together, roll it again, and cut out more cookies. Place cookies 1 inch apart on a parchment paper–lined baking sheet. Sprinkle 1 teaspoon granulated sugar on top of each and bake for 10 to 12 minutes. Transfer to a wire rack to cool before serving.

VARIATIONS

PÂTE SUCRÉE À L'ORANGE COOKIES
Add 1 tablespoon orange zest and 1 teaspoon orange extract to the flour mixture. Roll dough thinner, about ⅛ inch thick, before cutting out cookies.

PÂTE SUCRÉE AU CHOCOLAT COOKIES
Replace 2 ounces of the cake flour with 2 ounces cocoa powder. Roll dough thinner, about ⅛ inch thick, before cutting out cookies.

SWEETCRUST DOUGH RECIPES

APPLE TART LAYER CAKE

(1:3)

THE RECIPE This tart-turned-cake is inspired by Momofuku Milk Bar pastry chef Christina Tosi's apple pie layer cake. My version is made from thick, soft sweetcrust dough, cardamom diplomat cream (a mixture of pastry cream and whipped cream), apple spice pie filling, and a ginger crumble topping. It's one of my all-time favorite desserts.

THE RATIO This recipe is more filling and topping than dough—far more. And that's how it should be. It has a 1:3 ratio of dough to filling.

1. Position a rack in the center of the oven and preheat oven to 375°F. On a lightly floured surface roll prepared sweetcrust dough with a rolling pin to ¼ inch thick. With a large cookie cutter cut out 4 (6-inch) circles. Arrange circles on 2 parchment paper–lined baking sheets. Bake for 14 to 18 minutes, just until golden but still soft. Let cool on the baking sheets.

2. Assemble cake: Place one piece of baked sweetcrust on a plate. Spread one-quarter of diplomat cream on top followed by one-quarter of apple pie filling. Top with the next piece of sweetcrust and repeat, adding 3 more layers. Top the final layer of pie filling with ginger crumble and serve.

Cardamom Diplomat Cream

Pour ½ quart whole milk into a medium saucepan. Cut 1 vanilla bean in half lengthwise and scrape out seeds. Add seeds and pod to milk. Heat mixture over medium-high heat until it reaches the scalding point (180°F on a clipped-on thermometer).

Meanwhile, stir 1 ounce (¼ cup) cornstarch, 4 ounces granulated sugar, ¼ teaspoon salt, and 2 eggs in a large bowl. Pour one-third of the hot milk into egg mixture, whisking constantly, to temper. Pour tempered mixture back into saucepan. Bring to a boil over medium-high heat, stirring constantly. Cook for another 30 seconds and then remove from heat. Remove vanilla bean pod. Stir in

YIELD: 1 (6-inch) layer cake

PREP TIME: 3 hours

BAKE TIME: 18 minutes

2 pounds prepared Sweetcrust Dough (double the recipe on page 88)

1 quart Cardamom Diplomat Cream (recipe at left)

1 quart Opal Apple Pie Filling (page 93)

16 ounces Ginger Crumble (page 93)

continued on next page

1 ounce (2 tablespoons) butter and ½ teaspoon ground cardamom. Cover with parchment paper. Let cool to room temperature and then refrigerate for about 1 hour, until completely chilled.

While custard chills, whip 1 cup heavy cream with an electric stand or hand mixer on high speed. Once it begins to thicken, slowly add 2 ounces granulated sugar. Continue whipping until stiff peaks form. Fold whipped cream into custard and store in the refrigerator until ready to assemble cake. Yield: About 1 quart.

Opal Apple Pie Filling

Heat 2 ounces (4 tablespoons) unsalted butter in a large saucepan over medium-low heat. Add 3 pounds cored, peeled, and diced Opal apples. Cook, stirring occasionally, for about 10 minutes, until apples just begin to soften. Stir in 3 ounces granulated sugar, 3 ounces light brown sugar, ½ tablespoon lemon juice, 1 teaspoon ground cinnamon, ½ teaspoon ground cardamom, ¼ teaspoon ground dried ginger, and ¼ teaspoon salt. Raise heat and bring to a simmer. Cook for another 10 minutes, until apples are soft. Strain apples from liquid, reserving apples. Let cool before assembling cake. Yield: About 1 quart.

Ginger Crumble

Position a rack in the top of the oven and preheat oven to 375°F. Mix 4 ounces granulated sugar, 4 ounces light brown sugar, 4 ounces all-purpose flour, ¼ teaspoon ground dried ginger, ½ teaspoon minced fresh ginger, and ½ teaspoon salt in a large bowl. Add 2 ounces (2 tablespoons) cold unsalted butter. Pinch butter into sugar mixture with your fingers. The mixture should clump together easily. Spread crumble on a parchment paper–lined baking sheet. Bake for 10 to 12 minutes, just until golden. Let cool completely. Yield: About 16 ounces.

CHOCOLATE CHERRY TART

1:3

THE RECIPE Few foods go together as well as cherries and chocolate. And when you combine them with a few nutty walnuts and a little bright, fresh lemon zest, you have the perfect tart. The chocolate is in the dough rather than the filling, illustrating just one way you can modify a classic dough to suit your needs.

THE RATIO This recipe has a 1:3 ratio of dough to filling.

1. Preheat oven to 375°F. On a lightly floured surface roll sweetcrust dough with a rolling pin into a 12-inch circle about $\frac{1}{8}$ inch thick. Carefully push into a 9-inch round tart pan. Fold excess dough back down to sides, or trim. Line dough with aluminum foil and fill with pie weights or dried beans. Blind bake (see pages 73–74) for 10 to 12 minutes, until sides are set. Remove foil and pie weights. Poke holes in bottom of dough with a toothpick or fork and bake for another 12 to 15 minutes. Set aside to cool; keep crust in tart pan.

2. Pour filling into crust. Spread crumble evenly over the top. Bake for about 30 minutes, until top is light golden. Serve warm.

YIELD: 1 (9-inch) tart

PREP TIME: 1 hour

BAKE TIME: 30 minutes

1 pound Sweetcrust Dough, prepared with 2 ounces cocoa powder substituted for 2 ounces cake flour (see page 88 for instructions)

2 pounds cherry filling (double the filling recipe from Classic Cherry Hand Pies on page 63)

6 ounces Walnut Crumble (recipe below)

Walnut Crumble

Combine 4 ounces light brown sugar, 4 ounces granulated sugar, 1 ounce all-purpose flour, 4 ounces chopped walnuts, 1 teaspoon lemon zest, and $\frac{1}{2}$ teaspoon salt in a bowl. Cut 2 ounces cold unsalted butter into $\frac{1}{4}$-inch cubes and pinch into flour mixture with your hands until mixture is crumbly. Yield: 6 ounces.

VARIATION

DOUBLE CHOCOLATE TART Replace cherry filling with chocolate pastry cream (page 149) and top with Vanilla Whipped Cream (page 69) instead of walnut crumble.

MOON PIES

1:2

THE RECIPE This recipe comes from pastry chef Rebecca Masson, who (as she explains is typical for many pastries) adapted the recipe from another pastry chef, who likely was inspired by the creation of yet another pastry chef, and so on into history. Now's your chance to make it your own.

THE RATIO Though marshmallow is airy, these moon pies are doused in chocolate, giving them a 1:2 ratio of dough to filling.

1. Prepare sweetcrust dough according to the recipe on page 88, but reduce the cake flour to 2 ounces and add 2 ounces graham flour and 2 ounces whole wheat flour.

2. Preheat oven to 375°F. On a lightly floured surface roll dough with a rolling pin to to ¼ inch thick. With a 2½-inch round cookie cutter, cut out 16 cookies, kneading and rerolling dough as necessary. Place cookies on a parchment paper–lined baking sheet. Bake in the center of the oven for 8 to 10 minutes, or until cookies just begin to turn golden. Let cool on baking sheets.

3. Fill a pastry bag with marshmallow filling. Line another baking sheet with parchment paper and arrange half of the cookies, bottom side up, on it. Pipe a 1-inch-high mound of filling onto each, keeping it within ⅛ inch of the edge. Place remaining cookies bottom side down on each mound of filling and press down so filling protrudes slightly from between cookies. Let rest at room temperature for 30 minutes and then in the freezer for 30 minutes more.

4. Melt chocolate in a bowl over a large pot of simmering water. Stir in oil until mixture is blended and chocolate is thinned. Place a wire rack on top of a baking sheet. Remove cookies from the freezer. Dip each one into chocolate, coating completely in chocolate. Scrape any excess chocolate from the bottom cookie with a small icing spatula. Place coated cookies on the prepared wire rack. Return coated cookies to the freezer for 30 minutes to set chocolate.

YIELD: 8 (2-inch) moon pies

PREP TIME: 1 hour

BAKE TIME: 30 minutes

1 pound Sweetcrust Dough (page 88), prepared as below

2 ounces graham flour

2 ounces whole wheat flour

16 ounces Marshmallow Filling (recipe below)

8 ounces milk chocolate

2 teaspoons grapeseed or other flavorless oil

5. To remove set moon pies from the rack, lift one side of the rack and let it drop back to the counter to shake them loose, or slide a small icing spatula between the cookies and the rack to separate them. Serve or store in an airtight container in the refrigerator for up to 4 days.

Marshmallow Filling

Whip ½ cup egg whites (about 4 egg whites) in the bowl of an electric stand mixer fitted with a whisk attachment on medium-low speed until frothy. Mix ¼ ounce unflavored gelatin (1 packet) in 2 tablespoons cold water. Meanwhile, heat 8 ounces granulated sugar and ¼ cup water in a saucepan over high heat; when the temperature reads 230°F on a clipped-on thermometer, increase the mixer speed to high and whip egg whites to stiff peaks. Remove sugar from heat when it reaches 245°F. Stir gelatin into hot sugar until dissolved. Reduce mixer speed to medium and slowly pour hot sugar in a thin stream between the whisk and the side of the bowl, taking care not to let sugar hit the whisk. Increase the speed to high and whip for about 20 minutes, until mixture has cooled to room temperature and forms stiff peaks. Yield: 16 ounces.

PÂTE À CHOUX dough is a mechanically leavened dough that can expand when baked, leaving a large cavity in the center. It is the most unusual dough in this book, beginning as a roux (the same mixture of flour and butter used to make sauces) that cooks on the stove before being baked. Choux is also the only dough that can be—and in fact often needs to be—piped. The dough ratio is

6 FLOUR : 4 FAT : 8 LIQUID : ½ SUGAR : 7 EGG .

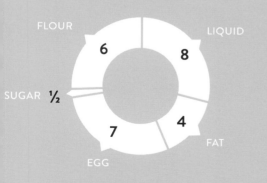

FLOUR · LIQUID · SUGAR · EGG · FAT

6 · 8 · ½ · 7 · 4

8 FLUID OUNCES WATER

4 OUNCES BUTTER

4 OUNCES BREAD FLOUR

2 OUNCES CAKE FLOUR

½ OUNCE SUGAR

4 EGGS

Use this dough to make:

Éclairs
Profiteroles
Gougères
Gnocchi

PÂTE À CHOUX DOUGH

| YIELD: 1 pound | PREP TIME: 30 minutes | BAKE TIME: varies |

4 ounces bread flour

2 ounces cake flour

½ ounce granulated sugar

½ teaspoon salt

1 cup water

4 ounces (8 tablespoons) unsalted butter

4 eggs

MAKING THE ROUX

1. Mix flours, sugar, and salt in a small bowl.

2. Heat water and butter in a medium saucepan over medium-high heat until butter is completely melted. Increase heat and bring to a boil.

3. Reduce heat to medium. Add flour mixture while stirring with a wooden spoon. Stir until mixture comes together into a ball.

4. Cook while stirring constantly, using the back of the spoon to press portions of mixture against the sides of the pot, for 1 to 2 minutes, until smooth.

MIXING THE DOUGH

Mix pâte à choux dough by hand or by using a stand mixer.

By-Hand Method

Place roux in a large bowl. Add eggs one or two at a time, stirring well with a wooden spoon after each until incorporated. Dough may not come together until after the last egg is added. Continue stirring until dough is elastic and matte in appearance.

Stand Mixer Method

Place roux in the bowl of an electric stand mixer fitted with the paddle attachment. Turn mixer to medium-low. Add eggs one or two at a time, letting them incorporate after each addition. Mix until dough is elastic and matte in appearance.

Qualities of a Good Choux

THE DOUGH: Pâte à choux dough should be elastic and fairly dry in appearance.

THE PASTRY: A good pâte à choux should have a crispy, hard shell and a large interior that is mostly empty except for a little eggy dough. If cutting baked dough in half and filling, you can remove this interior. If piping pastries, the filling will usually push these soft dough strands out of the way.

BUILDING PÂTE À CHOUX

Pâte à choux begins with a staple of French cooking, the roux. A cooked mixture of butter and flour, a roux often is used as a base for and to thicken sauces. To make a roux, add flour to a slow-boiling mixture of water and butter. Make sure the butter is completely melted before allowing the mixture come to a boil.

The roux needs to be dried out slightly for the baked pastry to achieve a good texture. To dry it out, use the back of a wooden spoon to push portions of the roux against the sides of a hot saucepan. Do this for 1 to 2 minutes.

Adding eggs makes the dough elastic and makes it expand during baking. Add the eggs one or two at a time with the pan off the heat. It is normal for the dough to come completely together only after the addition of the last egg. Continue mixing the dough until it forms elastic ribbons between the side of the bowl and the spoon or paddle attachment.

SHAPING PÂTE À CHOUX

This is the most fluid of the doughs, so it requires special shaping attention. The most common method is piping (see pages 102–103) although it can be scooped or spooned, especially when it will be fried in oil, as for beignets (page 111).

COOKING PÂTE À CHOUX

There are three basic ways to cook pâte à choux dough, each of which creates a different texture.

Baking

Pâte à choux is most commonly baked, which creates a large, hollow pastry with a crisp, crunchy exterior and almost nonexistent interior. The dough must be baked long enough at a relatively high temperature to form a hard shell, which will allow the pastry to retain its shape.

Frying

Deep-frying pâte à choux dough creates a large, tender, softer pastry with a paper-thin crispy exterior. It's not unlike frying brioche dough, though it requires a higher temperature (360°F) and a longer fry time (about 8 minutes) to crisp on the outside and fully cook on the inside.

Simmering

Simmering pâte à choux dough creates a dense, soft pastry. The dough cooks through but does not expand. After simmering it can be baked or pan-fried to give it a crispy exterior. This method is used to make gnocchi (page 113).

FILLING PÂTE À CHOUX

Fried or baked pâte à choux can be filled one of two ways: by simply cutting the pastry in half, scooping or piping filling into the center, and replacing the top; or by injecting the pastry with filling using a long, narrow piping tip. For more, see page 103.

PIPING ÉCLAIRS

1

Fit a large pastry bag with a ¼-inch circular tip (I use Ateco #802). Fill the bag with dough and twist the end shut.

2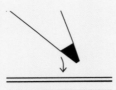

Hold the tip at a 45-degree angle to a parchment paper–lined baking sheet, about ½ inch from the sheet.

3

Apply constant, gentle pressure to the bag and move the tip and bag in a straight line, about 4 inches.

4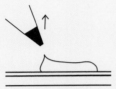

When you reach the end, stop applying pressure and lift the tip quickly. A small peak will form.

5

Dip your finger in water and push down the peak so it is flush with dough.

PIPING PROFITEROLES AND GOUGÈRES

1

Fit a large pastry bag with a ¼-inch circular tip. Fill the bag with dough and twist the end shut.

2

Hold the tip at a 90-degree angle to a parchment paper–lined baking sheet, about ½ inch from the sheet.

3

Hold tip in place and apply gentle pressure, letting a bulb form.

4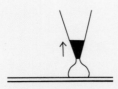

Once the bulb has reached the desired size, begin lifting the tip slowly.

5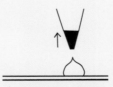

When the bulb reaches the desired height, stop applying pressure and lift the tip quickly. A small peak will form.

6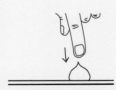

Dip your finger in water and push down the peak so it is flush with dough.

PIPING GNOCCHI

1

Fit a large pastry bag with a ¼-inch circular tip. Fill the bag with dough and twist the end shut.

2

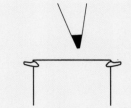

When you are ready to cook gnocchi, hold the bag over a pot of simmering water.

3

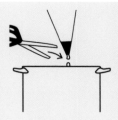

Apply pressure and cut dough every ½ inch with scissors.

FILLING PROFITEROLES

1

Slice profiterole in half.

2

Fill bottom half.

3

Replace top half.

FILLING ÉCLAIRS

1

Fit a pastry bag with a long, narrow piping tip.

2

Insert the tip into one end of éclair and apply pressure to the bag, filling the pastry.

PÂTE À CHOUX DOUGH RECIPES

SALTED CARAMEL ÉCLAIRS

1:4

THE RECIPE Éclairs are the quintessential pâte à choux, and although this pastry is common, it is often made incorrectly, resulting in a soft, deflated shell and chewy bite. Done properly, it has a crisp, crunchy exterior. Even better, this version has a filling far more interesting than the traditional Bavarian cream.

THE RATIO This recipe has a 1:4 ratio of dough to filling.

1. Preheat oven to 375°F. Pipe prepared pâte à choux dough into éclair shapes (see page 102) on a parchment paper–lined baking sheet spaced at least 2 inches apart. Bake for 45 minutes, until crust is golden brown and hard to the touch. Let cool to room temperature.

2. Pour pastry cream into a pastry bag fitted with a long, narrow piping tip. Inject the tip about ½ inch into the side of an éclair. Apply gentle pressure to the bag until pastry is full; the filling will begin to leak out around the tip. Repeat with remaining éclairs.

3. Drizzle caramel sauce over each éclair. Top with a few pieces of salted caramel popcorn, sprinkle with kosher salt, and serve.

YIELD: 16 pastries

PREP TIME: 2 hours

BAKE TIME: 45 minutes

1 pound prepared Pâte à Choux Dough (page 100)

8 ounces Salted Caramel Pastry Cream (page 107)

4 fluid ounces (½ cup) Caramel Sauce (recipe at left)

2 ounces Salted Caramel Popcorn (page 107)

1 teaspoon kosher salt

Caramel Sauce

Mix 8 ounces granulated sugar and 2 tablespoons water in a heavy-bottomed medium saucepan over high heat. Bring to a boil. Boil for about 15 minutes, until mixture is a caramel color. Remove from heat. Slowly, while stirring, pour in ¾ cup room-temperature heavy cream. Be careful because the caramel may bubble up or splash out. Add 2 ounces (4 tablespoons) chopped, room-temperature butter and stir until melted. Let cool until it is thick. Yield: About 16 ounces (2 cups) caramel, enough to flavor the pastry cream and popcorn (page 107) and drizzle over the assembled éclairs.

continued on next page

Salted Caramel Pastry Cream

Pour 2 cups whole milk into a medium saucepan. Cut 1 vanilla bean in half lengthwise and scrape seeds into milk. Add vanilla bean pod. Heat mixture over medium-high heat until it reaches the scalding point (180°F on a clipped-on thermometer).

Meanwhile, stir together 1 ounce (¼ cup) cornstarch, 4 ounces granulated sugar, and 2 eggs in a large bowl. Pour one-third of the hot milk into cornstarch mixture, stirring constantly, to temper eggs. Pour tempered mixture back into the saucepan. Bring to a boil over medium-high heat, stirring constantly. Cook for another few seconds.

Remove vanilla bean. Add 2 ounces (4 tablespoons) butter and stir until blended. Let cream cool to room temperature and then refrigerate until completely cool. Fold 8 ounces (1 cup) Caramel Sauce into cooled pastry cream. Yield: About 16 ounces (2 cups).

Salted Caramel Popcorn

Coat the bottom of a medium saucepan with 1 teaspoon vegetable oil. Add 2 tablespoons popcorn kernels, cover, and heat over medium-high heat until kernels begin popping. Move the pan back and forth over the heat so that kernels don't burn. When the pops are more than a second apart, remove pan from heat. Pour in 4 ounces (½ cup) Caramel Sauce and 1 teaspoon salt and toss to coat. Yield: About 2 cups.

TIP   *Serve éclairs, like all pâte à choux, immediately. These pastries absorb moisture from the filling and air, so the longer they're stored, the softer they'll become.*

VARIATIONS

CHOCOLATE HAZELNUT ÉCLAIRS Omit pastry cream, caramel sauce, and popcorn. Fill éclairs with Chocolate Hazelnut Filling (page 83) and top with Chocolate Sauce (page 109).

LEMON CURD ÉCLAIRS Omit pastry cream, caramel sauce, and popcorn. Fill éclairs with lemon curd and top with White Chocolate Sauce (page 109).

VANILLA BEAN ICE CREAM PROFITEROLES

1:4

THE RECIPE The profiterole is the éclair's little brother. Its small size makes it perfectly suited for pairing with a scoop of ice cream.

THE RATIO This recipe has a 1:4 ratio of dough to filling.

1. Preheat oven to 375°F. Pipe pâte à choux dough into profiterole shapes (page 102) spaced at least 2 inches apart on two parchment paper–lined baking sheets, up to 24 per sheet. Bake for 45 minutes, until crust is golden brown and hard to the touch. Let cool to room temperature.

2. Cut each profiterole in half horizontally. Place a scoop of ice cream on each base using an ice cream scoop. Replace tops. Spoon a small amount of chocolate sauce over each profiterole and serve immediately.

TIP *The majority of this recipe's prep time is necessary for the homemade ice cream to freeze overnight. After the ice cream is ready, these little puffs come together fairly quickly.*

YIELD: About 32 pastries

PREP TIME: 24 hours

BAKE TIME: 45 minutes

1 pound prepared Pâte à Choux Dough (page 100)

1 quart Vanilla Bean Ice Cream (recipe below)

2 cups Chocolate Sauce (recipe below)

Vanilla Bean Ice Cream

Pour 1 cup heavy cream and 1 cup whole milk into a large saucepan. Cut 1 vanilla bean in half lengthwise and scrape seeds into cream. Add vanilla bean pod to pot. Heat mixture over medium heat until it reaches the scalding point (180°F on a clipped-on thermometer).

Whip 8 egg yolks and 8 ounces granulated sugar in the bowl of an electric stand mixer fitted with a whisk attachment on high speed until light and fluffy. Temper the egg mixture: pour one-third of cream mixture into egg mixture while whipping on low speed. Pour tempered mixture back into saucepan. Return to medium heat and cook, stirring constantly, for about 5 minutes, until mixture is thick and coats a spoon. Don't let it get too hot or cook for too long; you don't want the eggs to cook.

Pour mixture into a large bowl, let cool to room temperature, and then refrigerate until completely cool, at least 4 hours. Process in an ice cream maker according to the manufacturer's instructions. Place in an airtight container and freeze overnight to harden. Yield: About 1 quart.

Chocolate Sauce

Bring ¼ cup plus 2 tablespoons whole milk, 2 tablespoons light corn syrup, and 2 ounces granulated sugar to a boil in a small saucepan over medium-high heat. Stir in 1½ ounces cocoa powder. Bring back to a boil, stirring continuously. Add 4 ounces chopped dark chocolate. Stir until chocolate is completely melted and sauce is uniform. Yield: About 1 cup.

To make White Chocolate Sauce: Omit the cocoa powder and replace the dark chocolate with 4 ounces white chocolate.

CINNAMON BEIGNETS

(**1:0**)

THE RECIPE These beignets are the result of deep-frying pâte à choux dough. Similar to baking, deep-frying is hot and slow enough to allow the dough to expand and form a hard shell that retains its shape. And like most pâte à choux recipes, beignets are best eaten right away—and by the dozen.

THE RATIO Beignets contain a sprinkling of cinnamon and sugar, making their ratio of dough to toppings nearly 1:0. Don't worry—they're still delicious.

1. Heat oil in a large pot over medium-low heat until the temperature reaches 360°F on a clipped-on thermometer; reduce heat as needed to maintain temperature. Mix sugar and cinnamon in a large bowl; set aside.

2. Scoop dough with a 1-ounce cookie scoop and drop into hot oil, just a few pieces at a time. Cook for 6 to 8 minutes, until lightly golden brown, keeping the oil at 360°F.

3. Remove beignets from oil and immediately toss in cinnamon mixture. Transfer to a plate to cool slightly before serving. Repeat with remaining dough. Serve warm.

YIELD: About 24 pastries

PREP TIME: 1 hour

COOK TIME: 10 minutes

1 pound prepared Pâte à Choux Dough (page 100)

1 quart vegetable oil

2 ounces granulated sugar

1 tablespoon ground cinnamon

DEEP-FRYING

The key to cooking beignets properly is the oil temperature. If it drops too low, the pastry will take longer to cook, absorbing more oil and attaining an unpleasant, greasy flavor. If the oil becomes too hot, the pastry will burn before the interior is fully cooked.

VARIATION

COFFEE CREAM–FILLED BEIGNETS Instead of tossing beignets in cinnamon sugar, dust them with powdered sugar and fill them with Coffee Pastry Cream: follow the instructions for Vanilla Bean Pastry Cream (page 148) but replace ½ cup of the milk with ½ cup freshly brewed coffee. Chill coffee cream before piping into beignets.

THYME GNOCCHI PARISIENNE

1:1

THE RECIPE This version of gnocchi parisienne is a great example of how you can flavor pâte à choux dough with herbs, cheeses, spices, and other mix-ins. Ingredients with more mass, such as cheeses, should not exceed one-quarter of the weight of the dough.

THE RATIO This recipe has a 1:1 ratio of dough to toppings.

1. Prepare pâte à choux dough according to the instructions on page 100, adding 1 ounce of the parmesan, thyme, and rosemary before adding the eggs. Place dough in a pastry bag fitted with a ¼-inch-diameter circular piping tip. Meanwhile, bring a large pot filled with at least 6 quarts water to a simmer over high heat, and then reduce heat to maintain a simmer.

2. Following the instructions for piping gnocchi (page 103), drop 1-inch pieces of dough into water. Cook for about 5 minutes. With a slotted spoon transfer gnocchi to a paper towel–lined plate and set aside.

3. Prepare sauce: Melt 4 ounces (8 tablespoons) of the butter in a large frying pan over medium heat. Add onions and cook, stirring frequently, for about 10 minutes, until translucent. Reduce heat to low. Add heavy cream and the remaining 2 ounces cheese. Cook, stirring frequently, for about 10 minutes, until sauce begins to thicken.

4. Heat the remaining 1 ounce (2 tablespoons) butter in another large frying pan or cast-iron pan over medium-high heat. Add gnocchi in a single layer, and cook, tossing or stirring frequently, for 3 to 5 minutes, until they begin to brown. Toss gnocchi with sauce and serve.

YIELD: 4 servings

PREP TIME: 1 hour

COOK TIME: 30 minutes

1 pound Pâte à Choux Dough (page 100), prepared as below

3 ounces parmesan cheese, shredded, divided

1 tablespoon fresh thyme, finely chopped

½ teaspoon fresh rosemary, finely chopped

5 ounces (10 tablespoons) unsalted butter, divided

1 white onion, thinly sliced

½ cup heavy cream

CHEDDAR GOUGÈRES

8:1

THE RECIPE These gougères are a savory application of pâte à choux dough. They retain choux's classic puffed-up shape and can be served alone or filled with countless savory fillings.

THE RATIO This recipe has an 8:1 ratio of dough to mix-ins.

1. Preheat oven to 375°F. Line a baking sheet with parchment paper. Prepare pâte à choux dough according to the instructions on page 100, adding cheese before adding eggs.

2. Transfer dough to a pastry bag fitted with a ¼-inch circular piping tip. Pipe dough into gougère shapes (page 102) spaced at least 2 inches apart on prepared baking sheet.

3. Bake for 45 minutes. Serve immediately.

YIELD: About 24 pastries

PREP TIME: 1 hour

BAKE TIME: 30 minutes

1 pound Pâte à Choux Dough (page 100), prepared as below

2 ounces cheddar cheese, shredded

BRIOCHE DOUGH is a naturally leavened yeast dough, similar to a bread dough, that is enriched with eggs, butter, and sugar. It is used to create a wide range of light, airy, and breadlike pastries, including cinnamon rolls, doughnuts, brioche à tête, and even bread. The dough ratio is **10 FLOUR** : **2 FAT** : **3 MILK** : **1 SUGAR** : **3½ EGG** .

EGG 3½

FLOUR 10

SUGAR 1

LIQUID 3

FAT 2

- **6** OUNCES BREAD FLOUR
- **4** OUNCES CAKE FLOUR
- **2** OUNCES BUTTER
- **3** FLUID OUNCES MILK
- **2** EGGS
- **1** OUNCE SUGAR

Use this dough to make:

Doughnuts
Cinnamon rolls
Brioche
Rolls
Bread

BRIOCHE DOUGH

| YIELD: 1 pound 4 ounces | PREP TIME: 6 hours | BAKE TIME: varies |

3 fluid ounces (6 tablespoons) whole milk

1 tablespoon active dry yeast

1 ounce granulated sugar

2 eggs, room temperature

2 ounces (4 tablespoons) unsalted butter, melted

6 ounces bread flour

4 ounces cake flour

1 teaspoon salt

MIXING THE DOUGH

Mix brioche dough by kneading it by hand or using a stand mixer.

By-Hand Method

1. Heat milk in a small saucepan over medium-high heat until it reaches the scalding point (180°F on a clipped-on thermometer) and begins to steam and look foamy. Remove from heat and let cool at room temperature to 115°F.

2. Warm a large bowl by running hot tap water over the outside. Transfer milk to warm bowl and stir in yeast for about 2 to 3 minutes, until completely dissolved. Stir in sugar, eggs, and butter until well combined. Add flours and salt. Stir with a spoon until dough begins to form.

3. Place dough on a lightly floured surface and knead dough with floured hands, taking care not to add too much flour. It will be very sticky at first. Knead for 10 minutes, until dough becomes slightly elastic and slightly less sticky, but still tacky.

Stand Mixer Method

1. Heat milk in a small saucepan over medium-high heat until it reaches the scalding point (180°F on a clipped-on thermometer) and begins to steam and look foamy. Remove from heat and let cool at room temperature to 115°F.

2. Warm the large bowl of an electric stand mixer by running hot tap water over the outside. Transfer milk to warm bowl and

stir in yeast for about 2 to 3 minutes, until completely dissolved. Stir in sugar, eggs, and butter until well combined. Add flours and salt.

3. Fit the mixer with the dough hook and knead on low speed for about 2 minutes, until dough begins to come together. Increase speed to medium-low and knead for about 10 minutes more, until dough begins to form a loose ball. It should be slightly elastic and sticky.

RISING THE DOUGH

1. With a spatula sprayed with nonstick cooking spray, or with lightly floured or buttered hands, transfer dough to a buttered proofing tub or large bowl. Cover with a kitchen towel and let rise at room temperature (ideally between 68°F and 88°F) for about 2 hours, until doubled in volume. (If dough doesn't rise, the yeast was not activated properly or is dormant. You will need to start a new batch.)

2. Punch dough down by pressing on it lightly to deflate it. Using your hands, knead it in the bowl a few times to redistribute the yeast. Cover with a kitchen towel and let rest for 20 minutes, to allow the gluten to relax. If desired, let it rise a second time at room temperature for about 2 hours, or in the refrigerator for 4 to 8 hours or overnight, punching it down again and letting it rest 20 minutes before shaping.

3. The dough is ready to be shaped (see pages 121–122). After it is shaped, it needs to proof, or rise at room temperature, covered with a kitchen towel, for about 2 hours, until it has nearly doubled in volume.

Storage

Yeast dough cannot be stored long-term or frozen. You may keep it in the refrigerator for up to 1 day before shaping; note that the longer it sits, the stronger the yeast flavor will be, because the yeast continues to ferment until it is baked. Baked brioche can be stored in an airtight container at room temperature for up to 2 days.

Qualities of Good Brioche Dough

THE DOUGH: Brioche dough should be smooth, elastic, and tacky to the touch.

THE PASTRY: Baked brioche should have a dark, crisp, chewy crust and a very soft interior with a compact, regular crumb.

HEATING THE MILK

We begin by warming the milk to the scalding point (180°F) and letting it cool. This process is necessary for the dough to rise and develop flavor, because heating deactivates a protease enzyme in milk that would otherwise retard and possibly kill the yeast.

FLAVORS IN BRIOCHE

Traditional brioche recipes often have a 2:1 ratio of flour to butter. This recipe does not share that ratio; it is enriched with additional egg, sugar, and liquid (here, milk). Brioche dough is traditionally allowed to rise twice, first at room temperature and then in the refrigerator. Letting the dough rise again in the cooler environment slows the rising process and allows the flavor to deepen. For most applications (such as cinnamon rolls, doughnuts, and braided loafs, in which the dough is loaded with nuts, fruits, and other flavorful ingredients), a single rise is adequate to create a delicious yeast-leavened dough that allows the mix-ins to shine. For a loaf or straight brioche rolls, the second, refrigerated rise will ensure a more flavorful stand-alone dough.

THE TWELVE STEPS TO YEAST DOUGH

In general, there are twelve steps to baking yeast-leavened doughs, such as brioche, croissant, and danish. Knowing them will help you understand how to create these doughs:

1. **Scaling:** The ingredients are prepared and measured to ensure precise control.

2. **Mixing:** The dough is mixed and kneaded to develop gluten and structure.

3. **Fermenting:** The dough is left to rise and ferment to develop flavor and an airy crumb.

4. **Punching:** The risen dough is deflated and quickly kneaded to redistribute the yeast, allowing fermentation to continue.

5. **Dividing:** The dough is cut or torn into numerous portions to make shaping easier.

6. **Preshaping:** Immediately after dividing, the dough is given the rough shape of the final pastry to make the final shaping easier.

7. **Resting:** The dough is left to rest to allow the gluten to relax, which makes it easier to work with.

8. **Shaping:** The dough is shaped into the final pastry form.

9. **Proofing:** The dough is allowed to rise one last time to develop flavor, shape, and crumb.

10. **Baking:** The dough is baked at the appropriate temperature for the appropriate amount of time to develop a caramelized crust and soft interior.

11. **Cooling:** The dough is allowed to cool completely to finish the cooking process and let the crumb settle.

12. **Storing:** The baked pastry is kept in conditions that will preserve its best quality.

RISING AND PROOFING

Letting the dough rise is vital to making any yeast-leavened dough. As the yeast ferments, it consumes the sugars in the dough (both the natural sugars found in flour and other ingredients and any sweeteners you've added) and expels carbon dioxide, which creates air bubbles. This process not only aerates and expands the dough, it adds flavor. Doughs that are left to rise more than once—or left to rise in a refrigerator, which slows the leavening but not fermentation—will typically have a yeastier, more developed flavor.

Proofing, or the final rise, which happens just before a yeast-leavened dough is baked, is a crucial step. Proofing affects crumb density, doughiness of the cooked pastry, and crust quality, and it creates the final shape of the pastry. Underproofing dough (not allowing it to rise long enough) will produce a baked good that is too dense; overproofing (letting it rise for too long) will cause the baked good to crack and maybe deflate. Most doughs should rise to just under two times their initial volume before baking (they will continue to rise in the oven) but some will rise more or less so follow each recipe carefully.

Using a Proof Box

This essential final rise is best done in a proof box, a container in which the temperature and humidity are controlled in order to encourage fermentation. But you can mimic the effect of a proof box simply by finding a warmer or cooler place in the house for your proofing. Here are a few ideas.

Oven: Preheat oven to 400°F for 30 seconds to 1 minute and then turn it off. The temperature inside the oven should be around 80°F. Place a bowl of hot water in the bottom of the oven and the dough on a baking sheet on a rack above the water. Let sit until dough has proofed. This method is handy if your kitchen is either very cold or very hot.

Container: Any container can be used as a proofing box as long as it can be closed on all sides. Mist the dough with water using a spray bottle and place dough in the container to proof. This method works well in rooms that are not too hot or cold.

Proof Bag: Place dough on a baking sheet and enclose the pan in a large plastic bag, such as a lightweight clear trash bag. Holding the top of the bag open, mist water into the bag with a spray bottle. Pull down the top quickly to trap the air, or blow into the bag just before pulling down the top and wrapping it under the baking sheet, creating a dome over the pan. Let sit until dough has proofed.

TIMES AND TEMPERATURES

Unlike other doughs, which tend to bake for the same time no matter how they've been shaped, brioche baking times vary widely. Both cinnamon rolls and the braided brioche loaf are baked at 400°F, but one needs 12 minutes and the other 40. Meanwhile, it takes only 4 minutes to deep-fry brioche dough in 340°F oil. Volume can be a strong indicator of baking times, but always consult the recipe for precise times and temperatures.

BRIOCHE BALL

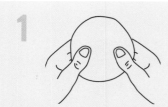
1 Gather dough into a ball. Touch your thumbs at the top of the ball and let your fingers support the bottom.

2 Move your thumbs apart, pulling dough with them, while using your fingers to push the excess inside.

3 Rotate ball 90 degrees and repeat until dough skin is taut.

BRIOCHE LOG

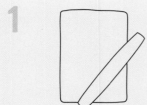
1 Roll dough into a rough rectangle.

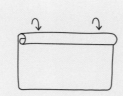
2 With your hands, roll dough into a tight spiral.

3 Push ends under the log by pinching them and tucking them under the log.

BRIOCHE À TÊTE

1

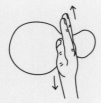

Using the side of your hand, roll dough ball into two balls, one a quarter the size of the other.

2

Push small ball into large ball, pinching around the edge of the smaller ball to keep it in place.

3

Carefully drop dough into a brioche pan.

CINNAMON ROLLS

1

Shape dough into a rough rectangle. Roll with a rolling pin into a thin, flat rectangle, longer or shorter as needed.

2

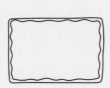

Spread filling over dough.

3

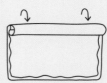

With your hands, roll dough over itself in a tight spiral.

DOUGHNUTS

1

Roll dough into a flat rectangle.

2

Cut out dough circles with a cookie cutter according to the recipe.

3

For classic doughnuts, use a ½-inch cookie cutter to cut out the centers.

BRAIDS

1

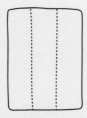

Shape dough into a rectangle and cut lengthwise into three equal strips.

2

Pinch ends together. Move the left strip over the center strip. Move the right strip over the new center strip. Repeat.

3

Pinch loose ends together and fold under loaf.

BRIOCHE DOUGH RECIPES

BRIOCHE À TÊTE

1:0

THE RECIPE The most common form of brioche, brioche à tête is named for its shape. *Tête* is French for "head" and in this pastry a small dough ball is placed on top of a larger one and then baked in a fluted pan. No fancy mix-ins here: serve with just a little jam or honey, and let the sweet, rich dough shine.

THE RATIO Brioche à tête is 100% dough.

1. Coat 8 brioche molds with nonstick cooking spray. Divide prepared dough in 8 equal portions and shape according to the brioche à tête method (page 122). Place dough in molds and place molds on a baking sheet. Cover with a kitchen towel and let proof for about 2 hours, until nearly doubled in volume (see Rising and Proofing, page 120, for more).

2. Preheat oven to 400°F. Brush brioches à tête with egg wash. Bake for 20 minutes, until tops are a dark, glossy brown.

3. Let pastries cool for a few minutes, until the molds are cool enough to handle. Turn brioches à tête in the molds on their side so air can circulate around them and let them cool completely before serving.

YIELD: 8 pastries

PREP TIME: 6 hours

BAKE TIME: 20 minutes

1 pound 4 ounces Brioche Dough (page 118), prepared but unshaped and unproofed

1 egg, beaten (egg wash)

VARIATION

HONEY-GLAZED DINNER ROLLS Form brioche dough into 9 balls (see page 121). Place balls in a parchment paper–lined 8-inch square pan. Cover balls and let proof for about 2 hours, until nearly doubled in volume. Brush rolls with a thin layer of honey and bake at 400°F for 20 minutes, until tops are a dark golden brown. Let cool, brushing with another thin glaze of honey while still warm.

CRANBERRY PISTACHIO BRAIDED BRIOCHE LOAF

2:1

THE RECIPE This recipe illustrates just how much brioche dough can hold—easily up to half its own weight in mix-ins. It is incredibly versatile: you can replace pistachios and cranberries with your favorite nuts and dried fruits, or omit them and replace the cardamom with other spices, such as cinnamon.

THE RATIO This recipe has a 2:1 ratio of dough to mix-ins.

1. Make brioche dough according to the directions on page 118, adding pistachios and cranberries along with the flour. Let rise once and then rest. On a lightly floured surface roll dough into a 12-by-6-inch rectangle. Brush lightly with egg wash; reserve remaining egg wash in the refrigerator. Mix sugar, cardamom, and salt in a bowl and sprinkle over dough.

2. Spray a 9-by-4-inch loaf pan with nonstick cooking spray or line with parchment. Cut dough into three 2-inch-wide strips but leave the top ¼ inch intact. Braid strips together (page 122). Place loaf in prepared pan, cover with a kitchen towel, and let rise for about 2 hours, until nearly doubled in volume. It should rise over the top of the pan by about an inch.

3. Position a rack in the center of the oven and preheat oven to 375°F. Brush dough lightly with the remaining egg wash and bake for 40 minutes, until crust is a dark golden brown. Let cool completely in the pan before serving.

YIELD: 1 (9-by-4-inch) loaf

PREP TIME: 6 hours

BAKE TIME: 40 minutes

1 pound 4 ounces Brioche Dough (page 118), prepared as at left

4 ounces roughly chopped shelled pistachios

4 ounces roughly chopped dried cranberries

1 egg, beaten (egg wash)

2 ounces granulated sugar

1 teaspoon ground cardamom

½ teaspoon salt

> ### VARIATION
>
> **CLASSIC BRIOCHE LOAF** Omit pistachios, cranberries, sugar, cardamom, and salt. After rolling the dough, leave it whole and roll it tightly on itself on the narrow end. Pull the curled ends down and pinch them under the bottom. Place loaf, pinched side down, in a 9-by-4-inch loaf pan. Rise and bake as above.

CINNAMON ROLLS

$(1:1)$

THE RECIPE I don't look forward to any breakfast pastry more than cinnamon rolls. Even though I can't imagine a less healthy breakfast dish—unless starting the day with a sugar rush is your definition of healthy—I still find myself clamoring for one of these soft, icing-covered confections in the morning.

THE RATIO Counting the glaze and the filling, cinnamon rolls have a nearly 1:1 ratio of dough to filling.

1. Line an 8-by-12-inch baking sheet or pan with parchment paper. Combine granulated and brown sugars, cinnamon, and nutmeg in a small bowl. On a lightly floured surface roll dough into an 8-by-12-inch rectangle. Position it with the long side nearest you. Brush with 2 ounces of the butter (it may pool in areas; that's fine) and sprinkle cinnamon mixture over top.

2. Roll into a log (see page 121). Slice into 12 equal portions: cut log in half, then cut each half in half, and finally cut each quarter into thirds. Arrange rolls in 4 rows on prepared sheet spaced at least 2 inches apart. Cover with a kitchen towel and let rise in a warm spot (between 68°F and 88°F) for about 2 hours, until rolls have doubled in volume and are touching.

3. Preheat oven to 400°F. Bake cinnamon rolls for 12 to 15 minutes, until crust is dark golden brown. Meanwhile, prepare glaze: combine the remaining 2 ounces butter, powdered sugar, vanilla, and 1 tablespoon water in a large bowl.

4. Let cinnamon rolls cool briefly, and then spoon glaze over them while still warm. Serve warm or let cool.

YIELD: 12 cinnamon rolls

PREP TIME: 6 hours

BAKE TIME: 40 minutes

1 pound 4 ounces prepared Brioche Dough (page 118)

2 ounces granulated sugar

2 ounces light brown sugar

½ tablespoon ground cinnamon

¼ teaspoon ground nutmeg

4 ounces (8 tablespoons) unsalted butter, melted, divided

8 ounces powdered sugar

¼ teaspoon vanilla extract

VARIATION

CHOCOLATE ORANGE BUNS Replace cinnamon and nutmeg with 4 ounces dark chocolate, finely chopped or shredded, and 1 tablespoon orange zest.

PB&J FILLED DOUGHNUTS

2:1

THE RECIPE Doughnuts are another wonderful application for brioche dough. Although I'm sometimes tempted to simply deep-fry a peanut butter and jelly sandwich, this PB&J-filled doughnut made with brioche dough is probably a better idea.

THE RATIO This recipe has a 2:1 ratio of dough to filling.

1. Line a baking sheet with parchment paper. Roll dough into a 6-by-8-inch rectangle. Cut out 6 circles with a 2½-inch round cookie cutter. Place circles on prepared sheet spaced 2 inches apart. Lightly press dough scraps together, forming a 2½-inch wide rectangle. Cut out 2 more circles and place on baking sheet. Cover with a kitchen towel and let rise for 1 to 2 hours, until about doubled in volume.

2. Line a plate with paper towels. Heat vegetable oil in a large pot until the temperature reaches 340°F on a clipped-on thermometer. With a slotted spoon carefully drop doughnuts into oil, working with a few at a time, making sure not to crowd the pot. Cook for 1 to 2 minutes, until golden on the bottoms. Flip with tongs and cook for another 1 to 2 minutes, until other sides are golden. Transfer to paper towel–lined plate. Repeat with remaining doughnuts.

3. Once doughnuts have cooled enough to handle, place peanut butter and grape jelly in separate pastry bags, each fitted with a long, circular piping tip. Slide the tip of one pastry bag about halfway into a doughnut and squeeze lightly to fill it halfway. Remove the bag. Insert the tip of the other bag about a quarter of the way through and squeeze lightly to fill the rest of the doughnut. Repeat with remaining doughnuts.

4. Dip the top of each doughnut in vanilla glaze. Transfer to a plate and sprinkle chopped peanuts (if using) on top. Let glaze cool and set slightly before serving.

YIELD: 8 filled doughnuts

PREP TIME: 6 hours

COOK TIME: 4 minutes

1 pound 4 ounces prepared Brioche Dough (page 118)

2 quarts vegetable oil

4 ounces Homemade Peanut Butter (page 131)

4 ounces Grape Jelly (page 79)

2 ounces Vanilla Doughnut Glaze (page 131)

4 ounces peanuts, finely chopped (optional)

Homemade Peanut Butter

You can make a nut butter with nearly any nut. Place 4 ounces peanuts in the bowl of a food processor. Process on the highest setting for 5 minutes, until peanuts turn into creamy paste. Yield: 4 ounces.

Vanilla Doughnut Glaze

Mix 4 ounces powdered sugar, 2 tablespoons whole milk, and ½ teaspoon vanilla extract in a bowl until smooth. Keep warm by placing bowl over a pot of simmering water. Yield: 1 cup.

VARIATION

CLASSIC GLAZED DOUGHNUTS Omit peanut butter, jelly, and peanuts. After cutting doughnuts, use a ½-inch round cookie cutter to cut a small hole in each. Let fried doughnuts dry on a paper towel for a few minutes. Dip the tops and bottoms in glaze. Let cool on a wire rack.

PUFF PASTRY dough is an unleavened pastry dough composed of flour, water, and butter. Two parts—a flour-based dough and a butter block—are stacked and folded using the double-turn technique, which keeps them from blending into a uniform mixture and creates hundreds of distinct layers. The dough ratio is **8 FLOUR** : **9 FAT** : **4 LIQUID** .

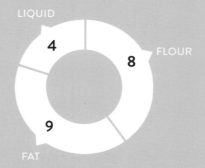

6 OUNCES BREAD FLOUR

2 OUNCES CAKE FLOUR

9 OUNCES BUTTER

4 FLUID OUNCES WATER

Use this dough to make:

Turnovers

Twists

Hand pies

Palmier

Mille-feuille

Tarte tatin

PUFF PASTRY DOUGH

| YIELD: 1 pound 4 ounces | PREP TIME: 4 hours | BAKE TIME: varies |

DOUGH

6 ounces bread flour

2 ounces cake flour

1 teaspoon salt

1 ounce (2 tablespoons) unsalted butter, melted

½ cup water

BUTTER BLOCK

8 ounces (1 cup) unsalted butter, cold

½ ounce bread flour

MIXING THE DOUGH

Combine flours, salt, butter, and water in a large bowl. Knead mixture, either with your hands or with an electric stand mixer fitted with a dough hook running on low speed, just until dough forms. Take care not to overmix. Shape dough with your hands into a rough 4-inch square. Wrap tightly in parchment paper and let stand at room temperature.

MAKING THE BUTTER BLOCK

There are two ways to make the butter block: kneading with your hands and using a stand mixer.

By-Hand Method

1. Working on a hard, cold surface (ideally a chilled marble slab) mash butter with the palm of your hand down and away from you to soften it. Gather the butter back together, rotate, and repeat until butter is soft and malleable but still cold. Add flour. Knead until well combined.

2. Shape mixture with your hands into a 6-inch square. Place between pieces of parchment paper. Roll into an 8-by-6-inch rectangle with a rolling pin. Refrigerate for about 30 minutes, until firm.

Stand Mixer Method

1. In the bowl of an electric stand mixer fitted with the paddle attachment, beat butter on low speed until it is broken up and

then increase to medium-high speed and beat until just softened. Add flour and mix on medium-high speed until combined.

2. With a spatula transfer mixture to a piece of parchment paper. Shape into a 6-inch square with your hands. Top with a second piece of parchment. Roll into an 8-by-6-inch rectangle with a rolling pin. Refrigerate for about 30 minutes, until firm.

MAKING THE DOUGH

1. Remove butter block from the refrigerator. Place dough on a lightly floured work surface and roll into a 12-by-8-inch rectangle, with the short side nearest you. Place butter block in center of dough (page 136). Fold top and bottom flaps of dough over butter block. Rotate dough 90 degrees and carefully roll into a 12-by-8-by-$\frac{1}{2}$-inch rectangle with a rolling pin.

2. Perform a double turn (page 136): Fold the top quarter of the dough down to the center. Fold the bottom quarter of the dough up, ensuring that it touches the edge of the top flap. Fold the two folded portions together, creating a 3-by-8-inch stack of folded dough. Gently press layers together. Wrap dough in parchment paper. Freeze for 25 minutes, until the dough and butter layers are about the same consistency (see Testing the Dough).

3. Repeat step 2 four more times, performing a total of five double turns and freezing for 25 minutes after each. After the fifth freeze, refrigerate for an additional 35 minutes before working with the dough.

Storage

Store dough wrapped in parchment paper or cling wrap. Refrigerator: 4 days. Freezer: 1 month.

Qualities of Good Puff Pastry

THE DOUGH: Puff pastry dough should be smooth and firm but easy to work with. Once the butter is folded into the dough, the dough and butter should remain the same consistency.

THE PASTRY: Baked puff pastry should be very delicate. It should rise high, and the interior should be flaky.

Testing the Dough

Before combining the dough and butter, lightly press your finger into each. The dough should provide resistance and spring back slowly—a small dimple will remain. The butter should deform slightly without cracking; you shouldn't, however, be able to easily press your finger more than ¼ inch into it. If the butter is too firm, leave it out for a few minutes. If it is too soft, refrigerate it. Do the opposite for the dough: refrigerate it if too soft, and leave it out if too tough.

To test whether the combined dough has chilled long enough, touch the surface. If it is tough and springs back quickly, let it rest longer in the refrigerator. If you create a deep dimple, the butter is too soft; back to the fridge with it. However, if the dough is very firm and no dimple forms, the butter is too hard—let it sit out room temperature for a few minutes.

BUTTER IN LAMINATED DOUGH

All laminated doughs—doughs that are created by folding layers of butter and dough together—are best made with butter that has a high butterfat content—at least 82%. During cooking the water in the butter evaporates into steam and leavens the dough. Butters with less butterfat contain more water, some of which may fail to evaporate. This impedes rise, and creates a doughy crumb.

MAKING A BUTTER BLOCK

Adding ½ ounce flour to the butter doesn't affect the overall ingredient ratio of this recipe, but it does make the dough easier to work with. To shape the butter block, roughly form it into a rectangle and then place it between two sheets of parchment paper and roll it into a thin rectangle. Then simply remove the top layer of parchment, flip the butter onto the flour dough, and remove the other sheet of parchment.

ENCLOSING THE BUTTER BLOCK

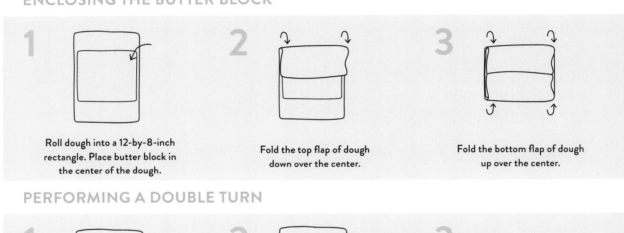

1 Roll dough into a 12-by-8-inch rectangle. Place butter block in the center of the dough.

2 Fold the top flap of dough down over the center.

3 Fold the bottom flap of dough up over the center.

PERFORMING A DOUBLE TURN

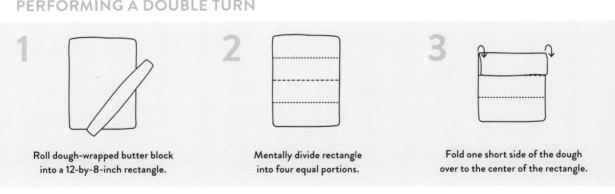

1 Roll dough-wrapped butter block into a 12-by-8-inch rectangle.

2 Mentally divide rectangle into four equal portions.

3 Fold one short side of the dough over to the center of the rectangle.

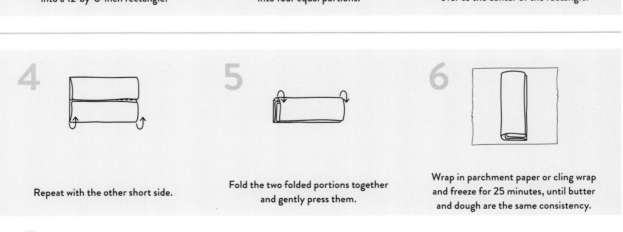

4 Repeat with the other short side.

5 Fold the two folded portions together and gently press them.

6 Wrap in parchment paper or cling wrap and freeze for 25 minutes, until butter and dough are the same consistency.

SHAPING PUFF PASTRY

Creating puff pastries in simple shapes is very easy. Roll the prepared dough on a clean work surface into a large sheet about ¼ inch thick. Let rest for 20 minutes. For squares, rectangles, and diamonds, use a sharp knife or a pizza cutter to cut straight lines. For circles, fluted squares, or unique shapes, use a large cookie cutter. For larger circles, place a small plate or dish on the dough and trace it with a sharp knife.

BAKING PUFF PASTRY

Puff pastry is baked at a high temperature—typically 400°F, but as low as 375°F and as high as 425°F—to ensure that the layers of butter cook out, creating the flaky texture.

PINWHEEL

1 Roll dough to ¼ inch thick. Let rest for 20 minutes. Cut out a 6-inch square. Cut 2-inch lines at corners as shown.

2 Fold half of each flap over itself, bringing the corners to the center to create a pinwheel shape.

TWIST

1 Roll dough to ½ inch thick. Let rest for 20 minutes. Cut out two 6-by-1-inch strips. Stack and pinch the ends.

2 Holding one end in place, twist the other end a few times to create a twist.

CONE

1 Roll dough to ¼ inch thick. Let rest for 20 minutes. Cut out a 12-by-1-inch strip.

2 Wrap the strip around the bottom of a cannoli cone and up the side, slightly overlapping the strip with each turn.

TURNOVERS

1

Roll dough to ¼ inch thick. Let rest for 20 minutes. Cut out a square.

2

Spread filling over one diagonal half of the square, leaving a ½-inch border.

3

Fold the other half over the filling and press the sides together with your fingertips.

ROSE

1

Roll dough to ¼ inch. Let rest for 20 minutes. Cut out a 6-inch square. Cut 2-inch lines from corners as shown.

2

Spoon filling into center. Fold up one cut-out flap and form into a petal shape circling the center.

3

Repeat with each flap, overlapping adjacent flaps to create a rose shape.

LATTICE-TOP HAND PIES

1

Roll dough to ¼ inch thick. Let rest for 20 minutes. Cut two rectangles. Spread filling over one, leaving a ½-inch border.

2

Cut a ½-inch strip from each side of the second rectangle. Cut the rest into diagonal ½-inch-wide strips.

3

Lay diagonal strips over filling as shown. Lay border strips along edges. Seal pastry shut.

POCKETS

1

Roll dough to ¼ inch thick. Let rest for 20 minutes. Cut out a rectangle.

2

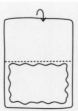

Spread filling over one half, and fold the other over. Crimp edges with a fork. Cut slits in the top.

PUFF PASTRY DOUGH RECIPES

GALETTE DES ROIS

$\boxed{2:1}$

THE RECIPE When I visited Paris, every pastry shop was selling a *galette des rois* (king cake), an edible celebration of Epiphany—nothing like the king cake eaten in the States. I ordered one within an hour of stepping off the plane. As soon as I tasted the flaky pastry and chocolate almond filling, I knew I had to make it myself.

THE RATIO This recipe has a 2:1 ratio of dough to filling.

1. Preheat oven to 375°F. Keep prepared puff pastry dough in the refrigerator while you prepare the filling: Cream sugar and butter in the large bowl of an electric stand mixer fitted with a paddle attachment on medium-high speed. Add 1 egg and almond extract and beat well on medium-high speed. Add chocolate and mix on medium-low speed until well combined. In another bowl combine flours and cocoa powder. Add to chocolate mixture and mix on low speed just until a thick batter forms.

2. Roll puff pastry dough into a 12-by-6-inch rectangle. Cut out two 6-inch circles. Beat the remaining egg. Brush one circle with egg wash and then spread filling on top, leaving a ¾-inch border bare around the edge. Top with the second dough circle and pinch the edges together with your fingers to create ridges.

3. With a paring knife cut a spiral of very shallow curved slits in the top of the pastry. Poke holes in the pastry to allow steam to escape during baking. Brush pastry with egg wash. Bake for 35 to 40 minutes, until dark, glossy brown. Let cool completely before serving.

YIELD: 1 pastry

PREP TIME: 30 minutes

BAKE TIME: 18 minutes

1 pound 4 ounces prepared Puff Pastry Dough (page 134), refrigerated

2 ounces granulated sugar

1 ounce (2 tablespoons) unsalted butter

2 eggs, divided

½ teaspoon almond extract

2 ounces dark chocolate, melted

1½ ounces almond flour

¼ ounce (4 teaspoons) cake flour

¼ ounce (1 tablespoon) cocoa powder

CHERRY PECAN MAPLE HAND PIES

8:3

THE RECIPE Puff pastry dough hand pies are similar to their less precise cousins, pie dough hand pies (see page 53). Forming them is simple: Place the filling on one half of a sheet of puff pastry, fold over the other half, crimp the edges, and cut steam holes in the top. Or get fancy and give it a lattice top!

THE RATIO This recipe has an 8:3 ratio of dough to filling.

1. Roll prepared dough into a 9-by-12-inch rectangle. Let rest in the refrigerator for 30 minutes.

2. Meanwhile, in a heavy-bottomed pot bring cherries, $\frac{1}{2}$ cup water, sugar, and lemon juice to a boil over medium-high heat. Lower heat and simmer for about 10 minutes, until just barely thickened. Reduce heat to low. Stir 2 tablespoons water and cornstarch in a small bowl until a paste forms. Stir paste into cherry mixture. Cook for another 30 seconds, until mixture thickens completely. Let cool.

3. Preheat oven to 400°F. Line a baking sheet with parchment paper. Cut dough into 12 (4-by-3-inch) rectangles. Place four rectangles on the prepared baking sheet. Spoon about $1\frac{1}{2}$ ounce (1 large spoonful) filling onto the center of each rectangle, leaving a $\frac{1}{2}$-inch border on the sides. Cut four of the remaining rectangles into $\frac{1}{2}$-inch diagonal strips. Arrange strips on top of filling to form a lattice top (page 138) on each pie. Cut the last four rectangles into strips and place them around the borders.

4. Brush dough with egg wash and sprinkle with chopped pecans. Bake for 20 to 25 minutes, until pastry has risen and is golden brown. Drizzle pies with maple syrup and serve.

TIP *For a simpler version, create puff pastry pockets or turnovers (see page 138). Can't find fresh cherries? This recipe works equally well with frozen cherries; thaw them completely before using.*

YIELD: 4 pastries

PREP TIME: 30 minutes

BAKE TIME: 18 minutes

2 pounds prepared Puff Pastry Dough (page 134)

$\frac{1}{2}$ pound fresh cherries, pitted and chopped

5 ounces granulated sugar

2 tablespoons lemon juice

1 ounce ($\frac{1}{4}$ cup) cornstarch

1 egg, beaten (egg wash)

Finely chopped pecans, for topping

Maple syrup, for serving

CRANBERRY ORANGE PUFF PASTRY POCKET Replace
cherries with $\frac{1}{4}$ pound pureed fresh cranberries, $\frac{1}{4}$ pound
chopped fresh cranberries, and 2 tablespoons grated orange
zest; cook as instructed at left. Form pocket as on page 138.

PUMPKIN SPICE HAND PIES Replace cherry filling with
pumpkin pie filling: Stir 8 ounces pumpkin puree (see
Homemade Gourd Puree, page 58), 1 ounce granulated sugar,
$\frac{1}{2}$ ounce ($\frac{1}{2}$ cup) cornstarch, 1 teaspoon ground cinnamon,
$\frac{1}{2}$ teaspoon ground nutmeg, $\frac{1}{4}$ teaspoon ground cloves, and
$\frac{1}{4}$ teaspoon salt in a bowl until well combined. This filling
does not need to be cooked before baking.

HONEY BOURBON GLAZED ALMOND PEAR TART

THE RECIPE A puff pastry tart is easier to make than a shortcrust tart because the crust doesn't require blind baking (see page 73). Simply top the puff pastry dough with a filling—in this case, pears poached in bourbon, honey, and brown sugar—and bake.

1:2

THE RATIO This recipe has a 1:2 ratio of dough to filling.

1. Roll prepared dough into a 10-by-4-inch rectangle. Let rest in the refrigerator for 30 minutes. In a large saucepan bring butter, sugars, honey, bourbon, lemon juice, and vanilla to a simmer over medium heat. Reduce heat as needed to maintain a simmer. Peel, core, and halve pears and carefully place cut side down in pan. Cook, covered, for 10 minutes. Meanwhile, preheat oven to 400°F and line a baking sheet with parchment paper.

2. Flip pears with a spoon, cover, and cook for another 10 minutes. Remove pears with a slotted spoon and set aside. Cover pot and bring liquid to a boil over medium-high heat. Reduce heat and simmer for about 10 minutes, until thick.

3. Place dough on prepared baking sheet. Arrange pear halves cut side down on dough. Sprinkle almonds on top. Drizzle with sauce to coat. Bake for 15 to 18 minutes, until puff pastry has risen and is golden brown. Let cool before serving.

TIP *Pears are more readily available in autumn, but this recipe can be made year-round with seasonal fruit. Try it with berries in the spring, plums or peaches in the summer, and apples in the winter.*

YIELD: 1 tart

PREP TIME: 40 minutes

BAKE TIME: 20 minutes

½ pound prepared Puff Pastry Dough (page 134)

2 ounces (4 tablespoons) unsalted butter

2 ounces granulated sugar

2 ounces light brown sugar

¼ cup honey

2 fluid ounces (¼ cup) bourbon

1 tablespoon lemon juice

1 teaspoon vanilla extract

2 large fresh pears

2 ounces sliced almonds

STRAWBERRY MINT PASTRY CIRCLES Roll 1 pound Puff Pastry Dough (page 134) to ¼ inch thick and cut out 4 (6-inch) circles. Spread 2 ounces (about 2 tablespoons) Vanilla Bean Pastry Cream (page 148) in the center of each circle, leaving a 1-inch border around the edges. Bake as above. Once cool, top with sliced strawberries and fresh mint leaves.

VANILLA BEAN PINWHEELS Roll 1 pound Puff Pastry Dough (page 134) to ¼ inch thick and cut out 4 (6-inch) circles. Shape dough into pinwheels (page 137). Fill center of each pinwheel with 2 ounces Vanilla Bean Pastry Cream (page 148). Brush with egg wash and sprinkle with ground cinnamon and granulated sugar. Bake as above.

CINNAMON TWISTS

5:1

THE RECIPE These twists are easy-to-make pastries that let their simple ingredients shine. Their spiraling shape offers plenty of surface area to be dusted with cinnamon and sugar, making every bite a sweet delight.

THE RATIO This recipe has a 5:1 ratio of dough to filling.

1. Preheat oven to 400°F and line a baking sheet with parchment paper. Roll puff pastry dough into a 12-by-8-inch rectangle. Cut rectangle into 12 (1-by-8-inch) strips and arrange strips on a lightly floured work surface. Brush with egg wash. Combine sugar and cinnamon and sprinkle over strips.

2. Twist two strips together tightly, pinching each end securely (see page 137). Place twist on the prepared baking sheet. Repeat with remaining strips.

3. Bake for 20 minutes, until twists are golden brown. Let cool completely before serving.

YIELD: 6 pastries

PREP TIME: 40 minutes

BAKE TIME: 20 minutes

1 pound prepared Puff Pastry Dough (page 134)

1 egg, beaten (egg wash)

2 ounces granulated sugar

1 tablespoon ground cinnamon

> VARIATION
>
> **PASTRY CREAM–FILLED PUFF PASTRY HORNS** After cutting dough into strips, wrap each strip around a metal cone mold and set on a baking sheet (see page 137). Bake at 400°F for about 20 minutes, until golden brown. Let cones cool before removing from the molds. Once completely cool, fill with Vanilla Bean Pastry Cream (page 148).

MILLE-FEUILLE

THE RECIPE Mille-feuille, also known as a Napoleon, is one of the best-known pastries made using puff pastry. Its alternating layers of vanilla diplomat cream and flaky pastry make for a rich dessert that plays with flavors and textures.

THE RATIO This recipe has a 1:1 ratio of dough to filling.

1. Preheat oven to 375°F. Roll prepared dough into a 12-by-8-inch rectangle. Pierce many holes in dough with a fork or toothpick to let steam escape during baking. (This is called docking the dough.) Transfer to a parchment paper–lined baking sheet. Bake for about 35 minutes, until dark golden brown. Let cool completely.

2. Meanwhile, prepare diplomat cream: in the large bowl of an electric stand mixer fitted with the whisk attachment whip heavy cream to soft peaks on high speed. Continue to whip while slowly adding granulated sugar. Whip to stiff peaks. Fold into Vanilla Bean Pastry Cream. Refrigerate.

3. Assemble mille-feuille: Carefully cut puff pastry into 3 equal pieces with a chef's knife. Spread half of the diplomat cream over one piece with a spatula. Top with a second piece of pastry. Top with remaining pastry cream followed by the third piece of pastry. Freeze for 30 minutes, until firm.

4. Cut frozen pastry into 4 slices. Let return to room temperature. Dust with powdered sugar and serve.

YIELD: 4 pastries

PREP TIME: 40 minutes

BAKE TIME: 35 minutes

1 pound prepared Puff Pastry Dough (page 134)

1 cup heavy whipping cream

1 ounce granulated sugar

2 cups Vanilla Bean Pastry Cream (see below)

Powdered sugar, for topping

Vanilla Bean Pastry Cream

Pour 2 cups whole milk into a medium saucepan. Cut 1 vanilla bean in half lengthwise. Scrape seeds out of pod with the tip of a paring knife. Add seeds and pod to milk. Heat milk over medium-high heat until it reaches the scalding point (180°F on a clipped-on thermometer) and remove from heat.

In a large bowl stir 1 ounce (¼ cup) cornstarch, 4 ounces granulated sugar, and 2 eggs. Slowly pour one-third of the milk into egg mixture, stirring constantly. Pour tempered egg mixture back into remaining milk. Bring to a boil over medium-high heat, stirring constantly. Cook for another few seconds.

Let cool to room temperature. Place plastic wrap or parchment paper on surface of pastry cream to keep a skin from forming. Refrigerate until cold. When ready to use, mix cold pastry cream by hand with a spoon until it thins and loosens, or use an immersion blender. Yield: About 2 cups.

To make Chocolate Pastry Cream: Add 4 ounces melted dark chocolate after cooking and stir.

ROUGH PUFF PASTRY (or quick puff pastry) dough is a mechanically leavened dough. It is made via the biscuit mixing method and a folding process that produces a flaky texture similar to that of puff pastry without the time commitment of the double-turn method. However, because it isn't a true laminated dough, it won't achieve the same rise as puff pastry. The dough ratio is

8 FLOUR : 8 FAT : 1 LIQUID .

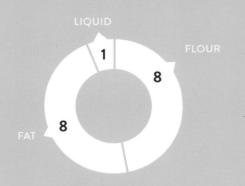

LIQUID
1

FLOUR
8

FAT
8

8 OUNCES FLOUR

8 OUNCES BUTTER

1 FLUID OUNCE WATER

Use this dough to make:

Turnovers

Twists

Hand pies

Palmier

Mille-feuille

Tarte tatin

ROUGH PUFF PASTRY DOUGH

| YIELD: 1 pound | PREP TIME: 45 minutes | BAKE TIME: varies |

6 ounces bread flour

2 ounces cake flour

1 teaspoon salt

8 ounces (1 cup) unsalted butter, cold

1 fluid ounce (2 tablespoons) water, cold

MIXING THE DOUGH

Mix rough puff pastry dough by hand or using a food processor.

By-Hand Method

Stir flours and salt in a large bowl. Cut butter into ½-inch pieces and add to flour mixture. Pinch butter and flour between your fingers until mixture is in large pea-sized chunks. Add water and stir with a spoon until dough begins to form.

Food Processor Method

Pulse flours and salt in the bowl of a food processor to combine. Cut butter into ½-inch pieces and add to flour mixture. Pulse, a few seconds at a time, until butter is broken into large pea-sized chunks. Add cold water while pulsing. Then pulse until a dough begins to form. Don't overmix.

ROLLING THE DOUGH

1. Transfer dough to a lightly floured surface. Roll with a rolling pin into a 12-by-8-inch rectangle. Perform a single turn, by folding dough into thirds like a letter (see opposite). Roll dough into a 12-by-8-inch rectangle again and repeat three more times, for a total of four single turns. (There is no need to let dough rest between turns.) Let dough rest in the refrigerator for 20 minutes.

2. Transfer dough to a lightly floured surface. Roll with a rolling pin into a 12-by-16-inch rectangle about ¼ inch thick.

Storage

Wrap in parchment paper or cling wrap. Refrigerator: 4 days. Freezer: 1 month.

Keep It Cold

Keep all ingredients and dough cold while working to ensure that the butter remains separate from the dough.

Qualities of Good Rough Puff Pastry

THE DOUGH: Rough puff pastry dough should be flexible and have visible chunks of butter, which will turn into streaks dispersed throughout the dough as it is rolled.

THE PASTRY: Baked rough puff pastry will be flaky and crumble easily, like pie dough, but will not have the rise of traditional puff pastry.

PERFORMING A SINGLE TURN

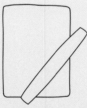

1 Roll dough into a rectangle with sides of roughly a 3:2 ratio (here, 12-by-8-inches), placing a short side nearest you.

2 Fold the top third (here, 4 inches) down over the center of the dough.

3 Fold the bottom third (here, 4 inches) up over the rest of the dough. Rotate 90 degrees before rolling again.

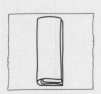

4 Wrap in parchment. If folding again (as for croissant or danish dough), rest first.

ROUGH PUFF PASTRY DOUGH RECIPES

SPICY MUSTARD SAUSAGE ROLLS

1:2

THE RECIPE One of my biggest guilty pleasures is hot dogs—I did write a cookbook all about them, after all—so it should be no surprise that I love this pastry variation. Take a big, plump, all-beef sausage, add some spicy mustard, and wrap it in flaky pastry, and you've got yourself the fanciest pig in a blanket around.

THE RATIO This recipe has a 1:2 ratio of dough to guilty pleasure.

1. Preheat oven to 350°F. Roll prepared rough puff pastry dough into a 12-by-8-inch rectangle. Cut dough into quarters, creating 4 (4-by-6-inch) rectangles. Cut each quarter in half diagonally to create 8 triangles.

2. Place one sausage link on the wide, short side of each piece of dough. Smear dough with mustard and tightly roll up the sausage. Place sausage rolls on a parchment paper–lined baking sheet. Brush with egg wash.

3. Bake for 20 minutes, until crust is golden brown. Let cool slightly before serving.

YIELD: 8 pastries

PREP TIME: 40 minutes

BAKE TIME: 20 minutes

1 pound prepared Rough Puff Pastry Dough (page 152)

8 (6-inch) beef sausage links

3 tablespoons spicy mustard

1 egg, beaten (egg wash)

GINGER APPLE TARTE TATIN

1:6

THE RECIPE Tarte tatin is the pastry version of upside-down cake. Apples or other fruits are boiled in sugar that then caramelizes. A layer of dough is placed on top. After cooling, the whole is flipped onto a serving dish. Try this recipe with nearly any fruit. Just reduce the cooking time if using a softer fruit: 30 to 40 minutes is best for pears, 20 to 30 minutes for berries.

THE RATIO This recipe has a 1:6 ratio of dough to filling.

1. On a lightly floured surface roll prepared rough puff pastry dough with a rolling pin into an 11-inch square and cut out a 10-inch circle using a pie plate or paper cut-out as a template. Transfer to a parchment paper–lined baking sheet, cover with a kitchen towel, and refrigerate.

2. Preheat oven to 375°F. Heat a 10-inch cast-iron or ovenproof stainless-steel skillet over medium heat. Add butter and let it melt. Add sugar and bring to a boil over medium-high heat, stirring constantly, for 2 minutes. Add apples, overlapping them so that there are no gaps between slices. (They will form a layer that holds up the pastry dough during baking.) Reduce heat to medium-low and continue cooking, without stirring, for about 10 minutes, until sugar caramelizes and turns a dark amber color. Sprinkle fresh and dried ginger and salt over apples.

3. Remove from heat and place pastry over apples all the way to the edges of the pan, ensuring that the edges don't drop down into apples. Bake for 40 to 50 minutes. The pastry will shrink a little and you'll be able to see the sauce bubbling.

4. Let pastry cool for 5 minutes. Run a knife along the inside edge of the skillet to ensure that nothing is sticking to the pan. Put a large plate upside down on top of the skillet. Quickly but carefully invert the pan so that the plate is on the bottom and pastry transfers to the plate. Remove skillet and replace any apples that fell out of place.

YIELD: 1 pastry

PREP TIME: 20 minutes

BAKE TIME: 50 minutes

1 pound prepared Rough Puff Pastry Dough (page 152)

6 medium firm apples, such as Pink Lady, peeled, cored, and quartered

1 ounce (2 tablespoons) unsalted butter

10 ounces granulated sugar

1½ teaspoons peeled and minced fresh ginger

1 teaspoon ground dried ginger

½ teaspoon salt

CROISSANT DOUGH is a laminated, naturally leavened dough that combines the yeast-leavened properties of brioche with the laminated properties of puff pastry. The proofing (to create light, airy texture) and turning (for the distinct layers) steps make this the most time-consuming pastry dough, but it's well worth it. The dough ratio is **10 FLOUR** : **7 FAT** : **6 LIQUID** : **¾ SUGAR** .

SUGAR
¾

LIQUID
6

FLOUR
10

FAT
7

12	OUNCES BREAD FLOUR	
8	OUNCES CAKE FLOUR	
14	OUNCES BUTTER	
12	FLUID OUNCES MILK	
1½	OUNCES SUGAR	

Use this dough to make:

Croissants
Pain au chocolat
Cinnamon rolls
Filled pastries

CROISSANT DOUGH

YIELD: 3 pounds	PREP TIME: 8 hours	BAKE TIME: 50 minutes

DOUGH

1½ cups whole milk

1 tablespoon active dry yeast

1½ ounces granulated sugar

2 ounces (4 tablespoons) unsalted butter, melted

12 ounces bread flour

8 ounces cake flour

2 teaspoons salt

BUTTER BLOCK

12 ounces (1½ cups) unsalted butter, cold

½ ounce bread flour

MIXING THE DOUGH

There are two ways to make croissant dough: kneading with your hands and using a stand mixer.

By-Hand Method

1. Heat milk in a small saucepan over medium heat until it reaches the scalding point (180°F on a clipped-on thermometer); it will begin to steam and appear slightly foamy. Remove from heat and let cool to 115°F at room temperature.

2. Warm a large bowl by running hot tap water over the outside. Add warm (105°F–115°F) milk to bowl and stir in yeast for about 2 to 3 minutes, until completely dissolved. Stir in sugar. Slowly pour in melted butter while stirring. Mix until homogenous. Add flours and salt. Stir until dough begins to form.

3. Transfer dough to a lightly floured surface and knead for about 2 minutes, until dough holds its shape and is smooth. Add flour to your hands and the surface as needed, but use as little as possible. Return dough to the bowl and let rest, covered with a kitchen towel, for 20 minutes.

4. Transfer dough to a lightly floured surface, ideally a large marble slab, and shape into a rough rectangle with your hands. With a rolling pin roll dough into a 12-by-16-inch rectangle. Carefully move to a parchment paper–lined baking sheet, cover with a kitchen towel, and let rest for 20 minutes.

Stand Mixer Method

1. Heat milk in a small saucepan over medium heat until it reaches the scalding point (180°F on a clipped-on thermometer); it will begin to steam and appear slightly foamy. Let cool to 115°F at room temperature.

2. Warm the large bowl of an electric stand mixer by running hot tap water over the outside. Add warm (105°F–115°F) milk to bowl and stir in yeast for 2 to 3 minutes, until completely dissolved. Stir in sugar. Slowly pour in melted butter while stirring. Mix until homogenous. Add flours and salt.

3. Knead with the electric mixer fitted with a dough hook on the lowest speed for about 1 to 2 minutes, until dough comes together and begins to form a smooth ball. Let dough rest in the bowl, covered with a kitchen towel, for 20 minutes.

4. Transfer dough to a lightly floured surface, ideally a large marble slab, and shape into a rough rectangle with your hands. With a rolling pin roll dough into a 12-by-16-inch rectangle. Carefully move to a parchment paper–lined baking sheet, cover with a kitchen towel, and let rest for 20 minutes.

MAKING THE BUTTER BLOCK

Make the butter block by kneading with your hands or using a stand mixer.

By-Hand Method

1. Using the heel of your palm, mash butter down and away from you on a hard, cold surface (ideally a chilled marble slab) to soften. Gather butter back together, rotate, and repeat, mashing butter until it is soft and malleable but still cold. Add flour. Knead until well combined.

2. Shape mixture into a 6-inch square with your hands. Place between pieces of parchment paper. Roll into a 12-by-10-inch rectangle with a rolling pin. Refrigerate for about 30 minutes, until firm.

Stand Mixer Method

1. Beat butter in the bowl of an electric stand mixer fitted with a paddle attachment until just softened. Add flour and mix.

2. With a spatula transfer mixture to a piece of parchment paper. Shape into a 6-inch square with your hands. Place another piece of parchment on top. Roll into a 12-by-10-inch rectangle with a rolling pin. Refrigerate for about 30 minutes, until firm.

MAKING CROISSANTS

1. Remove butter block from the refrigerator. Place dough on a lightly floured work surface with a short end nearest you. Place butter block on the bottom two-thirds of dough (closer to you). Fold the top, butterless third down over the center third. Fold the bottom third of dough and butter up over the rest (as if folding a letter into thirds). Wrap dough tightly in parchment paper or a kitchen towel. Place on a baking sheet and freeze for 25 minutes. If you need to let it rest longer, move it to the refrigerator.

2. Perform a single turn (see page 153): Unwrap dough and place on a lightly floured surface. Lightly pound dough with a rolling pin, starting from the center and working outward in both directions; start with the rolling pin parallel to the long side and repeat with it parallel to the short side. Flip dough and repeat. Once dough and butter have softened (see Testing the Dough, page 135), roll dough into a 12-by-16-inch rectangle, slowly and lightly so that the butter won't break. Fold dough into thirds. Wrap tightly and return to the freezer for 25 minutes.

3. Repeat the single turn (step 2) twice more, for a total of 3 single turns. Rest in the freezer for 25 minutes. Move to the refrigerator and rest for an additional 35 minutes.

4. Roll and shape according to recipe.

Storage

Croissant dough can be stored at various stages during folding, forming, and proofing. Cover with a kitchen towel or wrap tightly in parchment paper.

BEFORE FOLDING: Store the dough alone, before it and the butter block have been folded together. Refrigerator: 1 day.

AFTER FOLDING: Store after the dough and butter block have been folded 3 times. Refrigerator: 1 day. Freezer: 1 week.

AFTER SHAPING: Refrigerator: 1 day. Freezer: 1 month.

Qualities of Good Croissant Dough

THE DOUGH: Croissant dough should be very smooth. It should be the same thickness on all sides and corners. Any butter that is visible should remain intact and not broken, or in chunks dispersed throughout the dough.

THE PASTRY: Baked pastries should have a dark, crispy, flaky exterior that breaks easily. The interior should be softer, but chewy, with a somewhat irregular large crumb.

CROISSANT DOUGH BASICS

When making croissant dough, your kitchen should be cool (ideally between 60°F and 72°F). A cool environment is especially important while the dough proofs, because if the butter becomes too warm, it could leak out. Keeping the dough as cold as possible will also help the butter and dough layers stay separate.

We begin making croissant dough by heating milk to kill the enzyme that could retard the yeast, in order to ensure that the dough will rise efficiently and create a good crumb. Croissant dough shouldn't be kneaded more than is necessary to form it; each fold and turn in the laminating process will develop the gluten.

Pounding the dough before rolling it softens the butter and distributes it between the layers of dough, keeping it from breaking. When rolling this dough, take care to maintain its rectangle shape, especially at the corners, so that it folds and rolls evenly. Use just enough flour to keep the dough from sticking. Before folding, dust off any excess flour. If the dough resists being rolled, wrap it tightly in parchment paper and let it rest for 20 minutes in the refrigerator.

Don't skip or shorten the resting periods or rising times. Resting allows the gluten in the dough to relax and keep it cold. Rising lets the dough develop structure and flavor.

SHAPING CROISSANT DOUGH

These are the most common forms for croissant dough.

Simple Roll

The simple roll (opposite) is a rolled-up rectangle of dough that is a great vehicle for fillings and mix-ins.

Pain au Chocolat

Pain au chocolat (page 164) uses rectangular dough and is rolled from the sides to enclose chocolate.

Croissants

Croissants (page 164) are made with a triangular piece of dough that is rolled up to create the distinctive stepped look—traditional croissants should have three steps. And there are many stories regarding the rules of bending a croissant. I have most often heard that curved croissants are plain and straight ones have a filling. However, a recent pastry school graduate friend told me that their curved croissants were made with all margarine and straight with butter.

Baking Croissant Dough

Because of its high butter content, croissant dough requires a significant baking time to ensure that the butter evaporates completely. It may be tempting to take the croissants out early because of the browning of the crust, but be patient.

BUTTER IN CROISSANT DOUGH

Most of the butter in croissant dough is not incorporated; instead, it is laminated between layers of dough through turning. This helps the dough rise and creates a flaky, tender crumb.

WORKING WITH CROISSANT DOUGH

Croissant dough should be kept very cold while you work with it to ensure that the butter and dough layers remain separate. It should also be given plenty of time to rest between kneading, rolling, folding, and shaping to allow the gluten to relax, making the dough easier to work with. See Testing the Dough on page 135 for more.

PROOFING CROISSANT DOUGH

Croissant dough depends on the proofing periods in order to yield flavorful, properly shaped pastries. Because the dough is cold when you work with it, it requires a longer proofing time than other yeast-leavened doughs.

SIMPLE ROLL

1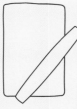
Roll dough into a long rectangle slightly larger than 8 by 18 inches. Trim with a sharp pairing knife to 8 by 18 inches.

2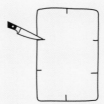
With a knife lightly mark the center of each short edge. Make a mark every 6 inches on the long edges.

3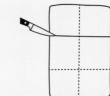
Connect the marks and cut along the lines, creating 6 (4-by-6-inch) pieces.

4
Stretch each piece of dough lengthwise to about 1⅓ its original length, about 8 inches.

5
Pinch one short end down on itself. Roll tightly, stretching and pulling dough. Turn so the seam is underneath. Repeat.

PAIN AU CHOCOLAT

1

Roll dough into a long rectangle slightly larger than 8 by 18 inches. Trim with a sharp paring knife to 8 by 18 inches.

2
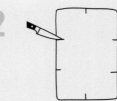
With a knife lightly mark the center of each short edge. Make a mark every 6 inches on the long edges.

3
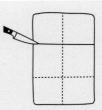
Connect the marks and cut along the lines, making 6 (4-by-6-inch) rectangles.

4

Stretch each piece of dough lengthwise to about 1⅓ its original length, about 8 inches.

5
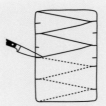
Pinch each short side down. Place a piece of chocolate next to each pinch.

6

Roll each short end to the center. Flip so pastry sits on the fold, which will keep it from unrolling during baking.

CROISSANT

1

Trim dough to 9 by 20 inches. Mark one side every 5 inches. Mark the other 2½ inches in and then every 5 inches.

2
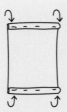
Connect the marks as shown. Cut along the lines. Cut a ¾-inch slit in the center of each short side.

3
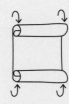
Carefully stretch dough to about 1⅓ its original length, 11–12 inches on the long side and 6–7 inches on the short.

4

For straight croissants: Pinch flaps down straight. Roll with the heel of your palm, while pulling the point taut.

5

For curved croissants: Pinch flaps down at an angle, toward one another. Roll as in step 4. Curl the ends toward the front.

6

Place croissants tip side down so that they don't unroll during baking.

CROISSANT DOUGH RECIPES

POOLISH CROISSANT DOUGH

Poolish croissant dough involves a few more steps than classic croissant dough; these steps are often used in bread baking to create a richer, more yeasty flavor. Fortunately, most modifications to the preparation simply involve increasing the various resting and rising times. During the additional poolish dough step, a portion of the dough is left to ferment before the rest.

YIELD: 3 pounds

PREP TIME: 2 days

BAKE TIME: 45 minutes

POOLISH

½ cup whole milk

½ teaspoon active dry yeast

4 ounces bread flour

1 ounce whole wheat flour

DOUGH

1 cup whole milk

2½ teaspoons active dry yeast

1½ ounces granulated sugar

2 ounces (4 tablespoons) unsalted butter, melted

6 ounces bread flour

8 ounces cake flour

1 ounce whole wheat flour

2 teaspoons salt

BUTTER BLOCK

12 ounces (1½ cups) unsalted butter, cold

½ ounce bread flour

1. Prepare poolish: Heat ½ cup milk in a small saucepan over medium heat until it reaches the scalding point (180°F on a clipped-on thermometer) and begins to steam and look foamy. Let cool to 115°F at room temperature. Transfer to a small bowl and stir in ½ teaspoon yeast for about 2 minutes, until completely dissolved. Stir in 4 ounces bread flour and 1 ounce whole wheat flour until a thick paste forms. Cover bowl with a kitchen towel and set in a warm (between 68°F and 88°F) place to rest for at least 8 hours.

2. Prepare dough: Heat 1 cup milk in a small saucepan over medium heat until it reaches the scalding point. Let cool to 115°F at room temperature. Transfer to the bowl of an electric stand mixer and stir in 2½ teaspoons yeast for about 2 minutes, until completely dissolved. Add sugar, melted butter, flours, and salt. Knead with the dough hook on low speed for about 1 minute, until dough begins to form. Add poolish. Continue kneading on low speed for about 1 to 2 minutes, until dough becomes smooth. Cover bowl with a kitchen towel and let rest for 20 minutes.

3. Move dough to a lightly floured surface and roll it into a 16-by-12-inch rectangle. Cover and let rest for 20 minutes. Prepare butter block and make croissants following the instructions beginning on page 161.

Because this dough can take more than 26 hours from start to finish, figuring out how and when to do each step can be tricky. Here are two sample schedules, one for baking croissants in the morning and another for baking them before dinner.

MORNING BAKE			
DAY 1		**DAY 2**	
8:00AM	Start poolish dough	8:00AM	Proof at room temperature
4:00PM	Knead dough	10:00AM	Bake
5:00PM	Begin turning dough		
8:00PM	Roll and shape dough. Proof overnight in refrigerator.		

EVENING BAKE			
DAY 1		**DAY 2**	
8:00PM	Start poolish dough. Leave out overnight.	8:00AM	Knead dough
		9:00AM	Begin turning dough
		10:00AM	Roll and shape dough. Proof overnight in refrigerator.
		4:00PM	Proof at room temperature
		6:00PM	Bake

CLASSIC BUTTER CROISSANTS

1:0

THE RECIPE If there is a quintessential pastry, the croissant is it. This is one of my favorite and most used recipes. I like to eat a croissant every day for breakfast. Sometimes it's an almond croissant, other times it's a savory ham and cheese croissant. Most often, it's this one: the classic butter croissant.

THE RATIO The classic croissant is 100% dough—the perfect example of how a dough can be great all on its own.

1. Shape prepared dough into croissants, as on page 164. Place on a baking sheet, evenly spaced so that they aren't touching, with the pointed ends underneath. Let rise in a proof box or bag (pages 120–121), spraying a light mist of water over them with a spray bottle every hour. Let rise for about 4 hours, until doubled in size and very soft. Pressing the dough should make a small indention that will not fill in.

2. Position a rack in the center of the oven and preheat oven to 425°F. Brush croissants with egg wash. Place baking sheet in oven and reduce heat to 400°F. Bake for 10 minutes, rotate the pan, and bake for another 15 to 20 minutes, until croissants have dark brown, glossy crusts, feel very light, and, if turned over, appear dry.

3. Let croissants cool on the baking sheet until they can be handled. Transfer to a cooling rack and let cool completely before serving.

TIP *If you prefer your croissants lighter in color, brush with beaten egg whites only, rather than an egg wash made from a whole egg.*

YIELD: 7 croissants

PREP TIME: 8 hours

BAKE TIME: 30 minutes

3 pounds prepared Croissant Dough (page 160)

1 egg, beaten (egg wash)

PAIN AU CHOCOLAT

16:1

THE RECIPE In this traditional preparation, two small chocolate bars are rolled up in croissant dough, creating the distinctive palmier look—along with a delicious chocolatey twist.

THE RATIO This recipe has a 16:1 ratio of dough to filling.

1. Shape prepared dough into pains au chocolat, as on page 164. Place on a baking sheet, evenly spaced so that they aren't touching, with the fold underneath each pastry. Let rise in a proof box or bag (pages 120–121), spraying a light mist of water over them with a spray bottle every hour. Let rise for about 2 to 4 hours, until doubled in size and very soft. Pressing the dough should make a small indentation that will not fill in.

2. Position a rack in the center of the oven and preheat oven to 425°F. Brush pastries with egg wash. Place baking sheet in oven and reduce heat to 400°F. Bake for 10 minutes, rotate the pan, and bake for another 15 to 20 minutes, until pains au chocolat have dark brown, glossy crusts and, if turned over, appear dry and feel very light.

3. Let pastries cool on the baking sheet until they can be handled. Transfer to a cooling rack and let cool completely before serving.

TIP *You can use any chocolate in this recipe. I prefer dark chocolate that is 60% to 70% cacao. If you cannot find small ½-ounce chocolate bars, cut 3 ounces dark chocolate into 12 small strips.*

YIELD: 6 pastries

PREP TIME: 8 hours

BAKE TIME: 30 minutes

3 pounds prepared Croissant Dough (page 160)

12 (½-ounce) dark chocolate bars

1 egg, beaten (egg wash)

CINNAMON ORANGE CROISSANT HONEY BUNS

8:3

THE RECIPE Cinnamon rolls (or honey buns, depending on your local lexicon) may be made from nearly any dough. Compared to brioche cinnamon rolls (page 129), which are softer and more delicate, these have a flaky, sturdy crumb. This recipe includes bright orange zest in the filling and a honey butter glaze on top.

THE RATIO This recipe has an 8:3 ratio of dough to mix-ins.

1. Line an 8-by-12-inch baking sheet with parchment paper and set aside. Bring butter, 5 ounces of the sugar, honey, corn syrup, and 1 tablespoon water to a boil in a small saucepan, stirring frequently. Boil for 1 minute. Set glaze aside.

2. Roll prepared croissant dough into a 12-by-16-inch rectangle on a lightly floured surface with the short side nearest you. Brush dough with just enough egg wash to coat; reserve remaining egg wash in the refrigerator. Sprinkle dough with the remaining 3 ounces sugar, cinnamon, and orange zest.

3. Working from the far side, carefully roll dough toward you, letting finished log rest on the crease to keep it from unraveling. Slice dough into 12 equal portions (cut dough in half, then cut each half in half, and finally cut each quarter into thirds).

4. Arrange rolls in 4 rows of 3 on the prepared baking sheet, spacing them about 1 to 2 inches apart. Cover with a towel and let rise in a warm spot (between 68°F and 88°F) for about 3 to 4 hours, until rolls have doubled in volume and are touching.

5. Position a rack in the center of the oven and preheat oven to 425°F. Brush rolls with egg wash. Place pan in oven, reduce heat to 400°F, and bake for 20 minutes. Rotate pan and bake for another 20 to 25 minutes, until crust is dark golden brown.

6. Let cool for a few minutes before serving. Spoon honey butter glaze over rolls while they're still warm.

YIELD: 12 cinnamon rolls

PREP TIME: 8 hours

BAKE TIME: 55 minutes

3 pounds prepared Croissant Dough (page 160)

2 ounces (4 tablespoons) unsalted butter, melted

8 ounces granulated sugar, divided

2 fluid ounces honey

1½ ounces light corn syrup

1 egg, beaten (egg wash)

1 tablespoon ground cinnamon

1 tablespoon grated orange zest (from ½ to 1 orange)

BLUEBERRY CROISSANT MUFFINS Roll dough into an 8-by-12-inch rectangle. Brush with egg wash. Sprinkle with 2 ounces granulated sugar and 4 ounces fresh blueberries. Roll and slice as above. Place each roll in the well of a greased muffin pan and let rise, covered with a kitchen towel or in a proof box, for 3 to 4 hours, until doubled in volume. Bake as above.

MAHÓN AND FELINO SALAMI CROISSANTS

12:1

THE RECIPE Croissants are perfect in that they can be adorned with any sort of topping or filling. They also can be sliced, filled, and eaten like sandwiches. This savory croissant takes the best of both worlds and bakes the sandwich fillings right in.

THE RATIO This recipe has a 12:1 ratio of dough to filling.

1. Shape prepared dough into croissants, as on page 164. After stretching the dough and before rolling, place a few pieces of salami and cheese on the top half of each triangle (near the short end). Carefully and tightly roll up each triangle. Place croissants on a baking sheet, evenly spaced so that they aren't touching, with the pointed ends underneath. Let rise in a proof box or bag (pages 120–121), spraying a light mist of water over them with a spray bottle every hour. Let rise for about 2 to 4 hours, until doubled in size and very soft. Pressing the dough should make a small indentation that will not fill in.

2. Position a rack in the center of the oven and preheat oven to 425°F. Brush croissants with egg wash. Place in the oven and reduce heat to 400°F. Bake for 10 minutes, rotate pan, and bake for another 15 to 20 minutes, until croissants have dark brown, glossy crusts and, if turned over, appear dry and feel very light.

3. Let croissants cool on the baking sheet until they can be handled. Transfer to a cooling rack and let cool completely before serving.

YIELD: 7 croissants

PREP TIME: 8 hours

BAKE TIME: 30 minutes

3 pounds prepared Croissant Dough (page 160)

2 ounces Felino salami, thinly sliced

2 ounces Mahón cheese, thinly sliced

1 egg, beaten (egg wash)

CHARCUTERIE AND CHEESES

Felino is a mild salami often flavored with garlic and white wine that comes from the town of Felino, Italy. It is typically 70% lean and can come from various scraps of pork, or "bench cuts." You can substitute any subtly flavored salami or even a cured pork such as capocollo.

Mahón cheese is a sharp, buttery, salty Spanish cow's milk cheese. You can substitute sharp, aged white cheddar or another creamy cow's milk cheese in these savory croissants.

> ### VARIATIONS
>
> **BROWN BUTTER AND BLACK PEPPER CROISSANTS**
> Omit salami and cheese. Sprinkle each triangle with a pinch of freshly ground black pepper before rolling. Brush croissants with brown butter (page 45) instead of egg wash before baking.
>
> **THYME AND SUN-DRIED TOMATO CROISSANTS** Omit salami and cheese. Sprinkle each triangle with 1 tablespoon finely chopped fresh thyme leaves and 2 ounces chopped sun-dried tomatoes before rolling.

DANISH DOUGH is a laminated, naturally leavened dough that has 243 layers when made with 4 single turns. It is similar to croissant dough except that it is enriched with eggs; it also undergoes an additional fold, which increases the number of laminated layers and gives it a lighter, softer crumb. The dough ratio is

10 FLOUR : **7 FAT** : **6 LIQUID** : **1 SUGAR** : **1⅓ EGG** .

SUGAR **1**

EGG **1⅓**

FLOUR **10**

LIQUID **6**

FAT **7**

	OUNCES CAKE FLOUR	Use this dough to make:
12	OUNCES CAKE FLOUR	Danishes
8	OUNCES BREAD FLOUR	Pockets
14	OUNCES BUTTER	Strudels
12	FLUID OUNCES MILK	Bear claws
2	OUNCES SUGAR	Combs
1½	EGGS	Twists
		Braids

DANISH DOUGH

YIELD: 3 pounds	PREP TIME: 8 hours	BAKE TIME: varies

DOUGH

1½ cups whole milk

1 tablespoon active dry yeast

2 ounces granulated sugar

1 egg, room temperature

1 egg yolk, room temperature

2 ounces (4 tablespoons) unsalted butter, melted

12 ounces cake flour

8 ounces bread flour

1 teaspoon salt

BUTTER BLOCK

12 ounces (1½ cups) unsalted butter, cold

½ ounce bread flour

MIXING THE DOUGH

There are two ways to mix danish dough: kneading by hand and using an electric stand mixer.

By-Hand Method

1. Heat milk in a small saucepan over medium heat until it reaches the scalding point (180°F on a clipped-on thermometer) and begins to steam and look foamy. Let cool to 115°F at room temperature.

2. Warm a large bowl by running hot tap water over the outside. Add warm (105°F–115°F) milk and stir in yeast for about 2 to 3 minutes, until completely dissolved. Stir in sugar, egg, and egg yolk until well combined. Slowly pour in melted butter, stirring continuously, until well combined. Add flours and salt. Stir until dough begins to form.

3. Pour dough onto a liberally floured surface. Knead, adding flour as needed, for 2 to 4 minutes, until it is smooth and holds its shape. Return dough to the bowl and let rest, covered with a lightly damp kitchen towel, for 20 minutes.

Stand Mixer Method

1. Heat milk in a small saucepan over medium heat until it reaches the scalding point (180°F on a clipped-on thermometer) and begins to steam and look foamy. Let cool to 115°F at room temperature.

2. Warm the large bowl of an electric stand mixer by running hot tap water over the outside. Add warm (105°F–115°F) milk and stir in yeast for about 2 to 3 minutes, until completely dissolved. Stir in sugar, egg, and egg yolk until well combined. Slowly pour in melted butter, stirring continuously, until well combined. Add flours and salt.

3. Knead with the dough hook on low speed for about 2 minutes, until dough comes together and begins to form a smooth ball. Let rest in the bowl, covered with a lightly damp kitchen towel, for 20 minutes. Line a baking sheet with parchment paper.

4. Transfer dough to a liberally floured surface, ideally a large marble slab. Shape dough ball into a rough rectangle. Roll dough into a 12-by-16-inch rectangle with a rolling pin. Transfer to prepared baking sheet, cover with a kitchen towel, and let rest for 20 minutes.

MAKING THE BUTTER BLOCK

Knead the butter block with your hands or use a stand mixer.

By-Hand Method

1. Using the heel of your palm, mash butter down and away from you on a hard, cold surface (ideally a chilled marble slab) to soften. Gather butter back together, rotate, and repeat, mashing butter until it is soft and malleable but still cold. Add flour. Knead until well combined.

2. Shape mixture into a 6-by-8-inch rectangle with your hands. Place between pieces of parchment paper. Roll into a 12-by-10-inch rectangle with a rolling pin. Refrigerate for about 30 minutes, until firm.

Stand Mixer Method

1. Beat butter in the bowl of an electric stand mixer fitted with a paddle attachment until just softened. Add flour and mix until combined.

2. Transfer mixture with a spatula to a piece of parchment paper. Shape into a 6-by-8-inch rectangle with your hands. Place another piece of parchment paper on top. Roll into a 12-by-10-inch rectangle with a rolling pin. Refrigerate for about 30 minutes, until firm.

MAKING DANISH DOUGH

1. Return dough to a lightly floured surface. Place butter block over the top two-thirds of the dough. Fold the bottom, butterless third up over the center third. Fold the top third down over the rest, like folding a business letter in thirds. Wrap dough tightly in parchment paper or a kitchen towel, place on a baking sheet, and freeze for 25 minutes. If you need to let it rest longer, move it to the refrigerator.

2. Unwrap dough and place on a lightly floured surface. Lightly pound dough with a rolling pin, starting at the center and working outward in both directions. Start with the rolling pin parallel to the long side and then repeat while holding it parallel to the short side. Flip dough and repeat until dough and butter have softened. (If you press on the dough, you should not feel hard resistance once your finger reaches the butter layer. If it is still tough, continue pounding.) Roll dough into a 12-by-16-inch rectangle, slowly and gently so that the butter doesn't break. Perform a single turn (see page 153) by folding dough into thirds like a letter. Wrap tightly and freeze again for 25 minutes.

3. Repeat step 2 three more times (for a total of four turns), letting dough rest in the freezer for 25 minutes. After the final freeze, let rest in the refrigerator for 35 minutes. Roll and shape according to recipe.

Storage

Danish dough can be stored at various stages during folding, forming, and proofing. Store it covered with a kitchen towel or tightly wrapped in parchment paper.

BEFORE FOLDING: Store the dough alone, before it and the butter block have been folded together. Refrigerator: 1 day.

AFTER FOLDING: Store after the dough and butter block have been folded 3 times. Refrigerator: 1 day. Freezer: 1 week.

AFTER SHAPING: Refrigerator: 1 day. Freezer: 1 month.

Qualities of Good Danish Dough

THE DOUGH: Danish dough should be very soft and smooth. It will be tacky before rolling and folding. It will remain soft throughout the turning process. It will require more flour than other doughs to prevent sticking.

THE PASTRY: Danish pastries should have a golden-to-brown, fairly crisp, flaky exterior crust and a soft interior with a dense but airy crumb.

Working with Danish Dough

Like croissant dough, danish dough should be kept very cold while you work with it to ensure that the butter and dough layers remain separate. It should also be given plenty of time to rest between kneading, rolling, folding, and shaping. See Testing the Dough on page 135 for more.

CROISSANT DOUGH VS. DANISH DOUGH

To the naked eye, danish dough will look similar to croissant dough. But there are a few important differences, which you can taste: Egg and sugar give danish dough richer, slightly sweeter flavor and a tenderer crumb. The flour ratio differs in these two doughs, as well: more cake flour and less bread flour give danish dough softer texture and crumb than croissant dough. Finally, because danish dough is turned one more time, it has more layers than croissants.

If you prefer the texture of croissant dough, feel free to substitute it in the recipes in this chapter. It pairs perfectly with the toppings and fillings.

BUTTER IN DANISH DOUGH

Most of the butter in danish dough is not incorporated into the dough; instead, it is laminated between layers of dough through turning, as in puff pastry dough and croissant dough. This butter helps the dough rise and creates a flaky, tender crumb.

PROOFING DANISH DOUGH

Like all yeast-leavened doughs, danish dough depends on the rising and proofing periods in order to yield flavorful, properly shaped pastries. See page 121 for tips on proofing dough.

SHAPING DANISH DOUGH

Danishes come in plenty of different shapes, many designed to hold fillings, such as classic open-faced circles, pockets, bear claws, strudels, and combs. Whatever the shape, danish dough is easy to work with when kept cold, given time to rest, and treated carefully.

OPEN-FACED CIRCULAR DANISH

1

Roll dough into a rectangle and trim with a sharp paring knife to exactly 12 by 18 inches.

2

Cut into 12 (1-by-18-inch) strips.

3

Twist one strip tightly. Roll strip into a circle, tucking ends under the center. Repeat with remaining strips.

DANISH POCKET

1

Roll dough into a rectangle slightly larger than 12 by 18 inches. Trim to exactly 12 by 18 inches.

2

Cut dough into 6 (6-inch) squares.

3

Fill the center of each dough square. Fold each corner over the center so the flaps overlap.

STRUDEL

1

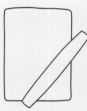

Roll dough into a rectangle slightly larger than 12 by 18 inches. Trim to exactly 12 by 18 inches.

2

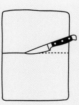

Cut into two 9-by-12-inch rectangles.

3

Make 11 (3-inch) cuts into each long side of the dough, creating 12 (3-by-1-inch) flaps on each side.

4

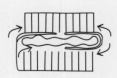

Place filling in the center of the dough. Wrap the four outer flaps inward to create a border.

5

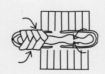

Overlap the remaining flaps, alternating sides.

BEAR CLAW

1 Roll dough into a rectangle slightly larger than 12 by 18 inches. Trim to exactly 12 by 18 inches.

2 Cut into 4 (9-by-6-inch) rectangles with a sharp knife.

3 Cut 4 (2-inch) slits into each long side, creating 5 flaps on each long side.

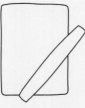

4 Place filling in the center of the dough in a ½-inch-thick line, leaving ¾ inch of space between the filling and the flaps.

5 Fold dough over, pinching flaps together to seal.

6 Fan flaps to create a half-circle bear claw.

COMB

1 Roll dough into a rectangle slightly larger than 12 by 18 inches. Trim to exactly 12 by 18 inches.

2 Cut into 4 (4½-by-12-inch) rectangles.

3 Make 11 (1½-inch) cuts into each long side of the dough, creating 12 (1½-by-1-inch) flaps on each side.

4 Place filling in the center, leaving ½ inch of space between filling and flaps.

5 Fold dough over, pinching flaps together to seal.

DANISH DOUGH RECIPES

CHERRY CHEESECAKE DANISHES

(2:1)

THE RECIPE   I first combined cherry and cheesecake filling in cinnamon rolls and immediately fell in love. I also quickly learned that trying to stuff cinnamon rolls with two thick fillings is a messy, difficult task. But danishes are a delicious and much easier vessel for this wonderful flavor combination.

THE RATIO   This recipe has a 2:1 ratio of dough to filling.

1. Shape prepared danish dough into 12 open-faced circular danishes (see page 181). Set aside, either on a parchment paper–lined baking sheet covered with a kitchen towel or inside a proofing box (see pages 120–121). Proof for 1 hour.

2. Preheat oven to 375°F. Place a small scoop of cheesecake filling and a small scoop of cherry filling in the center of each danish. Brush exposed dough with egg wash.

3. Bake for 35 minutes, until crust is golden brown. Let cool completely before serving.

Cheesecake Filling

Beat 8 ounces room-temperature cream cheese and 2 ounces granulated sugar until completely blended. Mix in $1/2$ ounce cornstarch (2 tablespoons) until completely incorporated. Mix in $1/2$ teaspoon vanilla extract and 1 egg until completely incorporated. Mix in 1 ounce sour cream until completely incorporated. Refrigerate until ready to use. Yield: 12 ounces.

Not only is this cheesecake filling great for danishes, it also works with nearly any pastry you can bake. In fact, you can use it to make a traditional cheesecake: double this recipe, pour it into a 9-inch crumb crust, and bake it at 350°F for 1 hour.

YIELD: 12 danishes

PREP TIME: 8 hours

BAKE TIME: 35 minutes

3 pounds prepared Danish Dough (page 178)

12 ounces Cheesecake Filling (recipe at left)

12 ounces cherry filling (from Classic Cherry Hand Pies on page 63)

1 egg, beaten (egg wash)

MAPLE BRAIDED DANISHES

THE RECIPE Maple syrup can be used for much more than just topping pancakes. I often add this versatile ingredient to cookie and cake batters, and I brush it on countless baked goods to add a unique, sweet flavor. Here it accents a simple pastry, allowing both the delicious dough and the syrup to shine.

THE RATIO This recipe has a 16:1 ratio of dough to filling.

1. Cut prepared danish dough into strips to shape into 6 braided twists. Before braiding, brush each strip with maple syrup and sprinkle with brown sugar and nutmeg; reserve any remaining syrup. Braid dough strips as on page 122. Proof for 1 hour.

2. Preheat oven to 375°F. Bake for 35 minutes, until golden brown.

3. If there is any maple syrup remaining, brush on pastries while still warm. Let danishes cool completely before serving.

TIP *This recipe works just as well with honey. Substitute your favorite variety for the maple syrup.*

YIELD: 9 danishes

PREP TIME: 8 hours

BAKE TIME: 35 minutes

3 pounds prepared Danish Dough (page 178)

⅓ cup maple syrup

1 ounce light brown sugar

½ teaspoon ground nutmeg

VARIATION

CRANBERRY PISTACHIO TWISTS Omit maple syrup. After cutting dough, brush with egg wash. Replace brown sugar and nutmeg with 2 ounces chopped dried cranberries and 2 ounces chopped pistachios. Twist dough (see page 137), transfer to a parchment paper–lined baking sheet, and sprinkle any toppings that have fallen out on top. Bake as above.

BERRY DANISH PINWHEELS

4:1

THE RECIPE When I make these danishes at home, I use homemade dewberry jam and top with whole dewberries. This berry is almost impossible to find, but—lucky for me—they grow naturally behind my house. Fortunately for everyone else, this recipe is perfect with nearly any berries, so choose those in season where you live.

THE RATIO This recipe has a 4:1 ratio of dough to filling.

1. Shape 6 danish squares according to step 1 of the pinwheel instructions (see page 137). Mix strawberry jam and cornstarch until well combined. Scoop a small spoonful of strawberry jam onto the center of each piece of dough.

2. Fold up the corners to create the pinwheel shapes, as in step 2 on page 137. Spoon a little more jam on top and top with blueberries and blackberries. Proof dough in a proofing box (see pages 120–121) or covered with a kitchen towel for 1 hour.

3. Preheat oven to 375°F. Bake for 35 minutes, until danishes are golden brown. Let cool completely before serving.

FRESH FRUIT VS. BAKED FRUIT

If you prefer fresh fruit on your pastries, you can add the berries after baking the pastries. Or you can do both.

> **VARIATION**
>
> **VANILLA PASTRY POCKET** Replace jam and berries with Vanilla Bean Pastry Cream (page 148). Shape dough into a pocket (page 181) instead of a pinwheel.

YIELD: 6 danishes

PREP TIME: 8 hours

BAKE TIME: 35 minutes

3 pounds prepared Danish Dough (page 178)

6 ounces Homemade Strawberry Jam (page 77)

½ ounce (2 tablespoons) cornstarch

3 ounces fresh blueberries

3 ounces fresh blackberries

APPLE STRUDEL

4:1

THE RECIPE This strudel combines the best qualities of apple pie and croissants. Larger than the typical single-serving danish pastries, it can hold a lot of the spicy apple filling—or any other filling in this book. So feel free to substitute another to suit your palate.

THE RATIO This recipe has a 4:1 ratio of dough to filling.

1. Preheat oven to 375°F. Shape prepared danish dough according to the strudel instructions (see page 181), filling each with 3 ounces (about ¾ cup) apple pie filling before folding.

2. Mix sugars and cinnamon in a small bowl. Brush top of pastry with egg wash and sprinkle cinnamon mixture on top.

3. Bake for 45 minutes, until crust is dark golden brown and filling is bubbly. Let cool completely before serving.

YIELD: 6 servings

PREP TIME: 8 hours

BAKE TIME: 45 minutes

3 pounds prepared Danish Dough (page 178)

12 ounces Apple Spice Pie filling (page 57)

1 ounce granulated sugar

1 ounce brown sugar

1 teaspoon ground cinnamon

1 egg, beaten (egg wash)

PHYLLO DOUGH is an unleavened dough famous for its paper-thin layers and flaky texture. Unlike laminated doughs (puff pastry, croissant, and danish), whose layers depend on a large percentage of butter in the dough, phyllo has almost no fat. It is instead rolled into separate layers that are then stacked before baking. The dough ratio is **32 FLOUR** : **12½ LIQUID** : **½ FAT** .

FLOUR
32

LIQUID 12½

½
FAT

32 OUNCES FLOUR

½ FLUID OUNCE OIL

12 FLUID OUNCES WATER

½ FLUID OUNCE VINEGAR

Use this dough to make:

Baklava
Phyllo stacks

PHYLLO DOUGH

| YIELD: 3 pounds | PREP TIME: 3 hours | BAKE TIME: 45 minutes |

2 pounds bread flour

½ fluid ounce white vinegar

½ fluid ounce vegetable oil

1½ cups water, very hot

MIXING THE DOUGH

Mix phyllo dough by hand or use a stand mixer.

By-Hand Method

1. Place flour, vinegar, oil, and water in a large bowl. Mix with a wooden spoon until dough is too tough to stir. Then mix dough with your hands until it holds its shape and no clumps remain.

2. Transfer dough to a lightly floured surface. Knead dough with the heel of your palm for about 15 to 20 minutes, working it until it is very elastic. The dough will be very tough.

3. Cover with a slightly damp kitchen towel and let rest for 1 hour.

Stand Mixer Method

1. Place flour, vinegar, oil, and water in the large bowl of an electric stand mixer fitted with the dough hook. Mix on low speed until dough begins to form.

2. Increase speed to medium-low and knead for 15 minutes, until dough is very smooth and elastic.

3. Cover with a slightly damp kitchen towel and let rest for 1 hour.

ROLLING THE DOUGH

1. Divide dough into 20 equal portions, by either cutting with a sharp knife or pulling pieces apart with your hands. Work with one piece of dough at a time, keeping the rest covered with a damp kitchen towel to keep them from drying out. Form dough

into a flat disk about 4 inches in diameter. Place on a lightly floured surface, such as a marble slab or cutting board. Place a rolling pin at the edge of the dough nearest you and roll away while firmly applying pressure. Rotate dough an eighth of a turn and roll again. Continue rolling and rotating, flouring the surface and rolling pin as needed, until dough is a circle about 8 inches in diameter.

2. Beginning with the rolling pin in the center of the circle, roll away firmly. Rotate dough a quarter of a turn and repeat. Continue rolling and turning until dough begins to resemble a rectangle. When dough begins to become very thin, use less pressure with each roll so that it doesn't tear.

3. Continue rolling, working one small section at a time, until you can begin to see the work surface through the dough. Be careful not to tear dough when moving or rolling it. When dough is roughly 10 by 12 inches, carefully lift it from the surface and place on a parchment paper–lined baking sheet. Top with another sheet of parchment paper.

4. Repeat with remaining dough, keeping the pieces you are not rolling covered with the damp towel. Stack on top of the baking sheet, separating each layer with parchment paper. Let rest for 1 hour before using.

Storage

Fresh phyllo will dry out quickly. If you plan to store it longer than one day, stack the sheets directly on one another, wrap in parchment paper or cling wrap, and freeze immediately. If using within one day, stack the sheets directly on one another on top of a lightly damp towel, cover with another lightly damp towel, and refrigerate. Refrigerator: 1 day. Freezer: 1 month.

Qualities of Good Phyllo Dough

THE DOUGH: Phyllo dough should be very tough and elastic. It will provide resistance when rolled, and it should roll very thin without breaking or tearing.

THE PASTRY: Once baked, phyllo dough should be very flaky and crumble easily.

Rolling Dough Paper Thin

Phyllo dough's defining characteristic is its paper-thin layers. And there are two keys to achieving those delicate sheafs: first, work the dough for a very long time to develop the gluten; and second, let the dough rest for a significant period of time before rolling to let the gluten relax completely.

Rolling the dough requires time and patience, because it must be rolled little by little. Working on a marble slab can help: the dough doesn't stick when it shouldn't, early in the rolling process, and it does when it's helpful, toward the end when you are rolling and stretching the dough. Once the dough becomes slightly translucent, you can stop flouring the surface.

ABOUT THE YIELD

For most applications, each sheet of phyllo, or one-twentieth of this recipe, can be cut in half after rolling and resting. This will yield 40 individual half sheets, which are large enough for most small-batch pastries.

WORKING WITH PHYLLO

It bears repeating: keep phyllo covered with a damp kitchen towel while you work with one piece at a time, so that this very thin, delicate dough does not dry out. When constructing a pastry with phyllo, any fillings, toppings, or sauces should be prepared ahead of time so that you can assemble the dish quickly. Brush melted unsalted butter between each layer of dough to hold the various layers together, add flavor, and create a crispy, flaky texture. Pastries made with phyllo dough should be baked right away.

HALF SHEETS

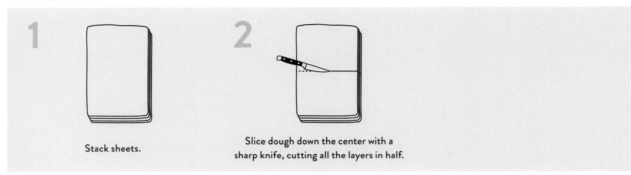

1 Stack sheets.

2 Slice dough down the center with a sharp knife, cutting all the layers in half.

BAKLAVA

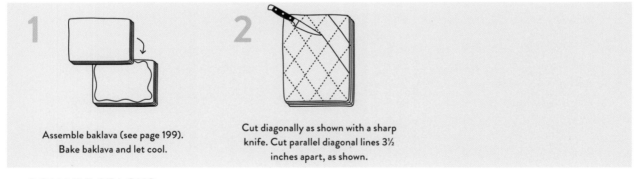

1 Assemble baklava (see page 199). Bake baklava and let cool.

2 Cut diagonally as shown with a sharp knife. Cut parallel diagonal lines 3½ inches apart, as shown.

SQUARE STACKS

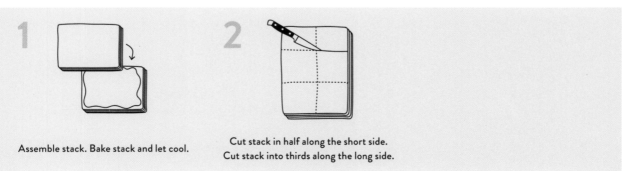

1 Assemble stack. Bake stack and let cool.

2 Cut stack in half along the short side. Cut stack into thirds along the long side.

PHYLLO DOUGH RECIPES

BAKLAVA

THE RECIPE Baklava is practically synonymous with phyllo. This pastry, which is believed to have originated in the Ottoman Empire, consists of layers of phyllo and chopped nuts under a honey glaze. It is rich, flavorful, and flaky—the makings of a truly perfect pastry.

THE RATIO This recipe has a 3:2 ratio of dough to filling.

1. Cut sheets of dough in half, resulting in 40 (10-by-6-inch) pieces. Cover with a damp kitchen towel. Preheat oven to 375°F.

2. Bring honey, cinnamon stick, and cloves to a simmer in a small saucepan over medium heat. Simmer for about 10 minutes, until liquid is reduced by one-third. Stir in orange zest and lemon zest. Let cool. Combine nuts in a small bowl.

3. Line a baking sheet with parchment paper. Place one sheet of phyllo over parchment and brush with melted butter. Repeat 9 times. Sprinkle one-third of the nut mixture evenly over the tenth sheet. Then stack another 10 sheets, brushing butter on each, and top with another third of the nut mixture. Repeat once more. After sprinkling the final third of nuts, stack the final 10 sheets of dough on top, still brushing each with butter.

4. Strain spices from syrup with a slotted spoon. Brush top of pastry with half the syrup.

5. Bake for 45 to 60 minutes, until golden and flaky. While still warm, brush pastry with remaining syrup. Let cool slightly before cutting into pieces (see page 196), and then serve.

MAKE IT YOUR OWN

Use different nuts and spices to customize this recipe. Try using all pistachios with a honey and lime zest syrup for a brighter flavor, or for a more intense flavor, combine chopped walnuts, pecans, and hazelnuts and use cinnamon, clove, and nutmeg in the syrup.

YIELD: 12 pastries

PREP TIME: 3 hours

BAKE TIME: 45 minutes

3 pounds prepared Phyllo Dough (page 194)

8 fluid ounces honey

1 cinnamon stick

4 whole cloves

1 tablespoon orange zest

1 teaspoon lemon zest

4 ounces pistachios, finely chopped

2 ounces walnuts, finely chopped

2 ounces almonds, finely chopped

8 ounces (1 cup) unsalted butter, melted

SUN-DRIED TOMATO STACKS

2:1

THE RECIPE These phyllo stacks are essentially a savory version of baklava: instead of chopped nuts and delicate honey syrup, they are packed with fresh herbs, balsamic vinegar, and a blend of cheeses.

THE RATIO This recipe has a 2:1 ratio of dough to filling.

1. Cut sheets of dough in half, resulting in 40 (10-by-6-inch) pieces. Cover with a damp kitchen towel. Preheat oven to 375°F.

2. Line a baking sheet with parchment paper. Place one sheet of phyllo over parchment and brush with melted butter. Repeat 9 times. Sprinkle one third of the sun-dried tomatoes, thyme, balsamic vinegar, and cheeses evenly over the tenth sheet. Stack another 10 sheets, each brushed with butter, and then add another third of the fillings. Stack 10 more sheets, add the final third of fillings, and finish with the final 10 sheets, brushing every sheet of dough with melted butter.

3. Bake for 45 to 60 minutes, until golden and flaky. Cut into squares (see page 196) and serve.

YIELD: 12 pastries

PREP TIME: 3 hours

BAKE TIME: 45 minutes

3 pounds prepared Phyllo Dough (page 194)

8 ounces (1 cup) unsalted butter, melted

8 ounces sun-dried tomatoes, roughly chopped

1 tablespoon fresh thyme, finely chopped

2 fluid ounces balsamic vinegar

4 ounces sharp cheddar cheese, grated

1 ounce Parmesan cheese, grated

INDEX

ABOUT THE AUTHOR

Russell van Kraayenburg, author of *Haute Dogs* (Quirk, 2014) and blogger at *Chasing Delicious*, is a self-proclaimed food nerd and pastry lover. His work has been featured in *Southern Living*, *Men's Fitness*, *Redbook*, *TRADhome*, *Real Simple*, and *Houstonia* magazines and on various websites including Lifehacker, Fast Co., Business Insider, The Kitchn, Live Originally, Quipsologies, Explore, and Fine Cooking. Russell is always looking for new and exciting ways to inspire food nerds and food-phobic individuals alike to pick up a whisk and spoon.

ACKNOWLEDGMENTS

Making a cookbook is not unlike constructing a well-prepared pastry. It's time-consuming and very rewarding, and old friends tend to come out of the woodwork wanting to be your taste testers. This book, as with some of the best pastries, took the time, dedication, and creativity of many hardworking, hungry people, all of whom I must thank—with more than just a few free pastries.

I first must thank the inventor of butter. Whoever first decided it was a good idea to spend hours hand-churning milk just to see what would happen is clearly a genius. Second, I have to thank my editor, Tiffany Hill, who had the difficult task of constantly reminding me that "1. Make the pastry." does not count as instructions for a recipe. I also want to thank Andie Reid for designing this beautiful book and the amazing team at Quirk for letting me ramble on about some of my favorite foods.

I must also thank my brother, Mason van Kraayenburg, and mother, Loree van Kraayenburg, for helping me create and style some wonderful photos for the book—and for not sending me a bill afterwards.

As for the recipes, they would not be possible without the guidance and help of three people. A special thanks goes to two pastry chefs with whom I have been working and studying this past year: Rebecca Masson of Fluff Bake Bar in Houston, and her number two, Kimberly Nguyen. Neither hesitated to answer any and all questions I had, and both were more than willing to go out of their way to show me the tricks of the trade that they learned from their teachers, and the teachers before them. Lastly, I must thank my friend Jonathan Lue-Tan who helped me test each and every recipe in this book. Without him, I would surely have been late(r) on each of my deadlines.